MW00936021

TWO FACE
OBLIVION

BY NICK VAN DER LEEK

"Do we not realize that self-respect comes with self-reliance?" — A. P. J. Abdul Kalam

Important Note to the Reader:

The *Rocket Science* books are unique. Throughout this book, the author has provided hyperlinks to relevant resources including documents, photographs and videos to enhance your interactivity with the story.

Disclaimer

On August 20 2018, Weld County prosecutors in Colorado formally charged Christopher Lee Watts with nine felony counts, including three counts of first-degree murder after deliberation [premeditated murder], two counts of first-degree murder in regards to victims under 12 in a position of trust, one count of first-degree unlawful termination of a pregnancy, and three counts of tampering with a deceased human body. As of this writing, November 2018, the defendant admits he murdered his pregnant wife, and pleaded guilty on November 6th to the murders of his two children. On November 19th 2018 Chris Watts was sentenced to multiple life sentences without the possibility of parole.

TABLE OF CONTENTS

Introduction

When Chris Watts left the computer room for lunch,* the door banged shut and the law enforcement trio were left to mull. And mull they did. While Watts sat down, picked up his spoon and started munching on macaroni, he had his morning session to contemplate [to himself]. Meanwhile two agents, one from the FBI [Grahm Coder] and one from the CBI [Tammy Lee] consulted with one another and with the lead detective from Frederick PD [David Baumhover].

During the break the three got to fine-tune their strategy and improve their respective approaches. They already had three hours of audio and some additional insight into the murders. They needed more.** Two could advise the third on how each could do whatever they were doing better. All three examined their notes and planned the next session using the first session as guidance. But it wasn't like they were interviewing Hannibal Lecter. It wasn't like Coder, Lee and Baumhover needed to use neurosurgery [or advanced psychology] to get into Watts' brain. They just had to *coax* their way in. Be nice to the guy. Don't be too pushy. And one of them could pick up the baton later in the conversation, if he dodged something, from the other.

When Watts returned, belly somewhat full and somewhat satisfied, *he* was primed and mentally prepared for the next session. But it was still one versus three, and no matter how sneaky Watts was, or how often he tried to feint away from questions, there was always going to be at least two fresh minds to take over the lead when the conversation [and mental evasion] stalled.

Three heads working against the cunning of Chris Watts, or rather, three crafty minds trained to deal with the criminal mind versus a mind way out of his depth once again, was at least twice as much mental firepower as Watts could muster. And just like it played out during the First Confession back in Frederick, Colorado, if the trio were patient and paced themselves, if they stuck to their respective strategies and played it just right, it would be like taking candy from a baby, wouldn't it?

*Lunch that day, February 18th, 2019, at Dodge Correctional was "macaroni and cheese, a bun, and some milk."

**In the chronology of the *CBI Report*, Shan'ann's murder and the murders of Bella and Celeste are recorded on pages 7 and 8, and 10 – 12 respectively. This implies that the entirety of the Second Confession [relating to the criminal acts themselves] occurred fairly early, during the first third of the discussion, before lunch and in two consecutive sets of disclosure. This is not the case. Some fragments of the confession were extracted during the first three hours, while other pieces of the puzzle had to be carefully pursued after the lunch break, as late as 3 hours 11 minutes into the 4 hour 40 minute interview.

TRUTH

"Better guilt than [truth and] the terrible burden of freedom and responsibility."—Ernest Becker, The Denial of Death

"Triggers"

"You never pull the trigger until you know you can win." — *Roger Ailes*

At exactly two hours and thirty minutes* into the four hour forty minute interview, Colorado Bureau of Investigation agent Tammy Lee asks Watts about "triggers". She mentions the torture of animals. She mentions his past, and asks Watts to imagine people speculating about him.

LEE: *You can imagine…Can you think back to the past at all, like, your childhood, and think about any other moments that maybe you [unintelligible] felt the same rage? I mean, obviously you didn't do anything like that but maybe felt that rage, and like…what…would have triggered that…or…anything like that?*

WATTS [Pregnant pause]: *Uh…not really. I mean I was always somebody that tried to coax people down.*

This part of the dialogue is referenced on page 20 of the *CBI Report*. Watts denies being triggered in his past by feelings of rage. It rings true, and that's a problem. The Watts Family Murders are brutal and violent. It does feel like rage, not only what he did but the callous disposal of their remains.

He carried them out of the house like trash...

And yet Watts himself doesn't seem violent even in his weakest moments. This is a contradiction that we will have to unravel in order to fully understand the man and the *why* and *how* of these murders. And this is the ambit of *OBLIVION*. How was a violent crime committed without violence? How was rage *not* an issue?

We begin our analysis by describing the problem. What is rage? Are we *sure* Watts is being truthful here about its absence back there in his background?

Rage is an aggressive, activating, confrontational emotion. Through hours of agonising interrogation [especially in August, including the long polygraph test] we hardly see any signs of pique, let alone rage. Throughout his interrogations Watts is well-mannered, even-tempered, polite and even friendly. Watts is never aggressive or confrontational to the cops, which is why they begin to adopt the same slow, cautious, gentle approach with him. Both sides begin to manipulate each other, but the cops accept the rules of the game since the premise gets Watts talking. Even if much of what he's saying is deceit, he's also leaking glimpses, and these glimpses can eventually be fashioned into a larger, more cinematic picture of the crime, and portrait of the criminal.

Uh...not really.

If Watts is authentic in his response it makes sense. It lines up with his backstory and what others have said about his character and personality as well.** <u>No one in his backstory has really accused Watts of violence or being hot tempered.</u>*** Shan'ann never did.

"I say things sometimes just to get him to react in <u>any</u> way since he doesn't react and that's not good...we have never ever fought. Literally

over anything serious. I have fought with him over stupid shit like not doing something I asked in a timely manner...[And I] did belittle him without realizing it with his parents. He's submissive when his parents are involved." – Shan'ann Watts to Addy Molony, August 12th, 2018, 09:04 [Discovery Documents, page 2115].

Actually, Watts is pretty submissive in general – to his parents, to his wife, to his children, to the media, to the cops, to the court that sentenced him...

Nichol Kessinger never saw Watts lose his temper either. If anyone got pissed it was her [or Shan'ann]. In fact Kessinger said she liked him precisely because he was so soft-spoken and even-tempered.

[Watts] was never hostile...He was always kind. To this day [Kessinger] said she didn't see any red lights...he's an introvert...he's reserved around other people. He...could get out of his shell [with her but not]... around most people....He was very relaxed all the time. He never really got worked up. They never had any arguments. He never lost his temper and she never saw him mad or upset. He was always very rational...He was not closed off. He was kind...They got along very well and [Kessinger] never got an indication that he was having issues. [Discovery Documents, page 2115].

He wasn't abusive to his children or his parents. It's simply *not there.* There's no trace of it in any of Shan'ann's social media. Even during Nut Gate, Watts' response to Shan'ann exploding at his parents is mild. There is a little evidence of arguing, one instance heard and seen on the driveway and another [or several others] overheard "flat-out screaming" by the neighbour.**** But who in the world has *never* argued with someone else, and which married person on God's green earth has *never* argued with their spouse?

The issue here isn't with Watts' answer but the CBI agent's question. The fact that CBI Agent Tammy Lee is looking for precedents of rage in Watts' backstory *suggests* she's nailed her colors to the mast of that particular emotion.*****

In the Second Confession Watts repeatedly makes the case that he *was* in a rage, that he snapped, felt the *epitome* of being angry, lost his mind, didn't know what happened, and wasn't in control. [*CBI Report*, four references feature on page 8 and one on page 12].

But rage *isn't* the operative emotion in this case. Rage isn't part of the emotional dynamic driving Watts. Remember Rourke saying during the sentencing hearing the crime was methodical and calculated?

"The defendant coldly and deliberately ended four lives…[looks up] not in a fit of rage, but in a calculated…manner."

That's not to say there are no feelings of anger or resentment, just that the *driving emotion* is something else.

When we look at Watts and listen to Watts, this contention seems less like insight than self-evident. The operative emotion with Watts seems to flow out of a sense of claustrophobia and suffocation. This is a crushed-in individual who doesn't have the confident sense of self to *be* himself. He can't be himself and perhaps he doesn't know how to be. When he is himself society punishes him. This is why the bisexual narrative is so sticky.

If Watts' sexual orientation is the elephant in the room, we can quickly and easily see why he's having difficulty being himself [especially within a marriage, the scenario of another baby on the way and the male-dominated industry that is oil and gas]. But if the bisexual narrative is a myth, then *what is his problem?* And if the operative emotion flows from these feelings of suffocation, what exactly is the operative emotion? If it's not rage, what the hell is it?

It's fear. But it's a particular sort of fear. It's a personal, private, idiosyncratic version of fear.

He feels suffocated by a society he can't understand, just as he feels suffocated by a marriage that doesn't feel right.

...he's an introvert...he's reserved around other people. He couldn't get out of his shell around most people...

His response to feelings of inadequacy and even humiliation is to withdraw into that shell and retreat into himself. But this only makes the world [including his marriage] more oppressive, more claustrophobic, more suffocating, not less. But retreating and hiding is what he does, so he defaults to it. He hides until there is no way out, and he finds himself trapped [by debt, by a pregnancy, by family dynamics].

But then something strange happens. Thrive happens. Watts begins to transform physically [outwardly] even if who he is only stirs a little. Then others notice him – like Kessinger. And then, out of the blue, pregnant Shan'ann and the kids depart from Colorado and the oppressive cloud lifts. The cage opens. And in that space beyond the bars, Watts briefly enjoys a giddy kind of freedom where he starts to not only glimpse himself but himself in a new life with a new wife and a whole other future.

It's important to juxtapose the phase of suffocation with the phase of freedom. What this does is it awakes in Watts an existential crisis. He has to make a choice. He has to choose who he wants to be, and what life he wants. He has to confront something. But he doesn't want to. He has to. But he doesn't want to. He can't. He won't. But then he does.

How does he do it?

Does he do it by losing his temper? Or does he do it the way he's always done things, by going into himself and finding a way, making a plan, preparing what to do and what to say? He's gotten away with hiding who is his whole life, so why would an invisible plan for an invisible crime not work?

The operative emotion driving Watts into the premeditation phase is *inadequacy*. It's a self-esteem thing. It's about an ego that doesn't think much of itself and – for the most part – allows people to walk all over him while he's in his head trying to figure it all out. This is why whenever we hear him speak Watts overdoes the hey-buddy charm offensive. It's a front, a mask of bravado designed to protect the vulnerable *other* Chris Watts hiding behind it.

But in the world of the unseen and the invisible, Watts isn't inadequate or insecure, he's just an introvert. In this secret world he's the kind. He's the only one who knows the finest details, not only about others, about locations, dates, numbers, machines and chemicals, but about himself.

*"I'm not used to not having a relationship with my dad. I should've just called him before it got to this point where **it got in my head.** I didn't and that's my fault."* – Chris Watts to Shan'ann on August 5th, 2018, referring to his passivity in the face of Nut Gate [Discovery Documents, page 2102]

Kessinger undoubtedly does *something* to Watts' ego, something his ego had never experienced before. Whatever she did, she let the cat out of the bag, so to speak. During their secret affair she revealed a secret side to Watts, but she also lit a fire under his sense of inadequacy, and under his ego. The raging furnace isn't rage, it's a fire of insufficiency, and the desire to fill it.

The ego is a symbolic construct for the self. This construct can be small in some cases, or colossal in others. Strangely, the greater the sense of self [the lower the levels of insecurity, or inadequacy], the less the ego comes to the fore. Think of individuals that should have big egos but don't, like Bill Gates and Neil Armstrong]. When the self is under attack, no matter whether the self is insecure or not, the ego is the first to respond. If the response is not to respond, in other words if there is an inward reply, then the reply comes from the ego, and the ego begins to expand commensurate to the threat. The longer this secret dialogue continues between the external and a man's interior world, the more the ego swells, balloons, until it begins to engulf the whole self.

The mainstream misperception of this case conflates the superficial impression of Watts as a musclebound monster, an immediate, reactive, narcissistic individual, with a violent crime. Yes, it was a violent crime. Strangling someone to death *is* an aggressive, physically confrontational and active method of committing triple murder for a man who is almost none of these things.

So if Watts is truthful, and if our psychology is on point, how was a violent triple murder committed *without* violence?

*The lunchbreak on February 18, 2019, at Dodge Correctional occurred approximately 30 minutes after this point in the discussion, at the three-hour mark in the audio clip. Since the investigators entered the prison at 07:45 [according to the *CBI Report*], on the face of it, it seems possible and even likely that the team spent as long as an hour setting up the room with recording devices. This is besides the administration and processing required when entering the prison premises. This scenario suggests a midday mealtime of 12:00, which seems reasonable, right? However, a cursory study of the Dodge Correction Institute's *RECEPTION STATUS HANDBOOK* [March 2018 revised edition, page 19] indicates three early <u>mealtimes</u>: **06:30** in the morning, **11:00** for lunch and dinner at **16:00**. This timeline somewhat counterintuitively indicates a quick entry and an apparently casual approach to setting up the room, a process that possibly took less than fifteen minutes if the interview started at 08:00 sharp. It should also be noted that the audio, as in other releases, may not be fully complete or may be partially redacted, censored or – for unknown reasons – removed. In any event, just as the chronology of the *CBI Report* does not always correspond to the actual chronology of the discussion, for storytelling efficiency and effectiveness, *OBLIVION* makes use of the same narrative license.

**Watts' long-time friend David Colon described Watts in a letter as "mild-mannered". In the same letter Colon noted:

"Come to think of it I don't ever remember [him] getting mad, yelling, cussing or anything..." [Discovery Documents, page 1977].

***Watts' supervisor at Anadarko, Luke Epple, said he has never seen him lose his temper at work. [Discovery Documents, page 560].

****<u>Nathaniel Trinastich overheard several confrontations</u> between Shan'ann and Chris Watts.

*****Although it seems the agents are playing dumb, and seem to suspect Watts had rage issues leading up to the murders, and accept that rage was a factor at the time, what they're really trying to do is get confirmation from him so they can <u>exclude the possibility of an unpremeditated attack</u>.

Watts in a Word

"Have you never known a cruel wind?...I never tease, madam! I coax, I beguile, I stomp...I am the shiver of the world! But I do not tease. You can cause ever so much more trouble by taking folk seriously, asking just what they're doing and doing just what they ask." — Catherynne M. Valente, The Girl Who Soared Over Fairyland and Cut the Moon in Two

What does Watts mean by:

I was always somebody that tried to coax people down.

Coax is an unusual, colorful word. When last did you use it? It's not a word I use often, not in my daily life and not often in the over 80 narratives already written. I'm not sure if I've ever used it in the hundreds of blog posts on *CrimeRocket*. Watts himself is hardly a bookworm or wordsmith himself, so this word is worth looking at. The superficial meanings of coax are:

Cajole

Charm

Sweet-talk

When we see Watts making his reluctant appearances in Shan'ann's Thrive videos, he tries to **cajole** the Facebook flock, trying to sound upbeat like all the other promoters. It's just not how Watts is. He's not a talker or a performer. Shan'ann on the other hand is a talker, is a performer, and seems to do very well at "cajoling" her captive audience, which is to say promoting her stuff and selling it. She may not have made much of an income out of it, but relative to the MLM community as a whole, Shan'ann was one of its stars, wasn't she?

We don't have much evidence of Watts **charming** Kessinger except we know that he did. We can't see much of what he said, but we know what he said was effective. We get a sense of Watts as a charmer in the Sermon on the Porch and in his initial sparring with Coder. In fact, Watts is such a nice guy neither the media nor the FBI agent seem to be willing to push him with really tough questions. When Watts wiggles out of a question or dodges a nudge they let him off the hook *because he's a nice guy.*

Whatever we may say about Watts' rusty social skills, he did **sweet-talk** Shan'ann into getting off track in terms of her initial intentions to divorce him and play hardball. Although he was distant, he knew when to sweet-talk his wife and thus influence her and bring her under his spell.

All three of these scenarios [cajoling on Facebook, charming the cops, sweet-talking his wife] are a kind of sly coaxing, aren't they? All three scenarios are subtle efforts to lie, deceive and influence an outcome.

While relevant, we cut to the meat of things when we apply the word coax to *a strategy for murder.* Remember our question at the end of the last chapter?

How was a violent triple murder committed without violence?

Answer:

I was always somebody that tried to coax people down.

But in the murderous sense, coax may begin with charming, sweet-talking and cajoling. As a strategy for murder we look to other meanings of the word.

These:

Inveigle

Entice

Lure

Inveigle has to do with gaining access to something or someone through trickery and deception. As socially awkward as Watts was leading up to the murders, he seemed to do better than Kessinger at hiding his adulterous communications, and generally covering his tracks. He also did well hiding the affair from apparently everyone for at least six weeks. And this same skill at inveigling reappears in the disturbing context of carrying out dead bodies on a driveway [invisible even though on camera] and disposing them before dawn in a way that no one expects let alone understands.

Entice has to do with seduction, and perhaps Kessinger is a better model to demonstrate its effects than Watts. But Watts himself "enticed" those around him with his numeracy, earning him the *Rain Man* moniker, and by hook or by crook, making himself more alluring to Kessinger than his male and in some cases also-married co-workers at Anadarko. There is also the enticing that goes along with Thrive. The word entice is associated with evil, and vanity and vice, but it uses psychology [temptation, dangling a carrot] to achieve its malevolent ends. When Watts describes Shan'ann killing the kids, or her disappearance simply because she left home in a huff, he's enticing the listener with a scenario that's superficially believable but untrue.

Lure. This is really the essence of what he means by coaxing.

I was always somebody that tried to coax people down.

On page 597 of the Discovery Documents, leading up to the polygraph examination on Wednesday August 15th, 2018, the word "lure" is volunteered by Watts. Once again, like coax it's a somewhat unconventional word in the true crime lexicon. This is where and how it comes up:

[Lee] explained to [Watts] that a person could physically cause another person's disappearance by murdering them...[Lee] asked [Watts] to list all the physical ways a person could cause someone's disappearance through murder.

Lee is trying to mindfuck Watts here, but it wouldn't be hard for Watts to register that. The mindfuckery is really Watts knowing he is being mindfucked [ahead of the polygraph test] and how he responds. *How well does he lie?* So when the now convicted murderer is asked to suggest the different ways of murdering someone, Watts isn't very imaginative or forthcoming – at first.

[Watts volunteered]: Stab someone, shoot someone, hit 'em with a blunt object, um, what else is there, I mean, use a weapon of like a gun or a knife.

Lee notes in her report that Watts "appeared to be thinking". She's asked him a simple question and he's really scratching his head thinking about it. Effectively then, he's thinking about what not to say, and perhaps how to appear if he does. Since Watts doesn't offer anything else, Lee prods him:

...I said, "You could smother someone." [Watts] repeated what I said and I immediately said, "You could strangle someone."

Watts says at this point it's difficult to think about "that kind of stuff right now". Lee prods him with more possibilities.

"A person could drown, shock, or burn someone to death..." [Lee] asked Watts if he could think of any other ways to murder someone and he said, "<u>Lure them into a trap</u>, I guess."

When Lee asks Watts to explain this, he has a very clear and very specific scenario:

*...he said you could have someone **waiting around the corner** and **an accident** could happen, such as **getting hit** by a car.*

If you think about it, it doesn't make any sense. How does waiting around a corner and a car accident have anything to do with luring? The answer lies in the word *wait*. The luring involves waiting **out of sight** for the right moment, thus <u>premeditation</u>.

Doesn't the act of murder, of dying, in this instance *also* involve waiting? Because the one scenario missing from all those mentioned here is *poison*. And <u>poison</u> and <u>chemicals</u> fits perfectly with a *spiel* of silently and invisibly coaxing, luring and inveigling. It's death as an <u>accidental overdose</u> unless the <u>overdose wasn't accidental</u>. It's a death and disposal in the real world that's not violent or confrontational, or even aggressive. What it is is sly, sneaky and cowardly, the personification of the Silver Fox.

Glimpses of Childhood from Behind Bars

"My childhood did not prepare me for the fact that the world is full of cruel and bitter things." —J. Robert Oppenheimer

The first two chapters are undoubtedly reductionist. Anyone can jump into over four hours of audio and handpick a nugget, and – in a vacuum – turn it into the Holy Grail of this case. That's not what we want to do. We don't want to be *too selective*, surgically removing only the relevant fragments that suit us while ignoring those that don't. We have to make the whole fit in order to advance the story, in order to find our way to the *OBLIVION* of why.

If the first chapters focused on one sentence in the Second Confession, as well as the single instance the word "lure" crops up in almost 2000 pages of discovery, as we move further into *OBLIVION*, we want to expose ourselves to a lot more, without too many interruptions or analysis, and see where the dominoes fall.

Worth playing for?

<u>WATTS</u>: *...I was not somebody who would fight somebody else. I think I had a fight like when I was in the third grade, but it was like...*

we ripped each other's shirt and went away crying. You know, it was like stupid.

LEE: *Mmhmmm.*

WATTS: *I was just like: Why-why did I...why did I do that? So...I can't think of anything.*

LEE: *Mmhmm. [Pressing him]. Did you feel it on the inside...even though you didn't act it out? Did you feel like...like if someone bullied you at school or someone...or whatever...would it still be inside you, like...? Did you feel like that even though you didn't actually act on it?*

WATTS: *I mean...I was always...because I didn't really talk to people, so I was...I never...People knew who I was but they didn't really...I mean I never had a girlfriend in high school. I was always just like...just flying under the radar.*

That's what Watts is doing here, now, in prison. That's what his <u>plea deal</u> is. Instead of a trial Watts would prefer just to go straight to prison and fly under the radar. What does this psychology – of flying under the radar – reveal about his choice of strategy to commit murder? Once again we see the idea of a non-confrontational, non-aggressive, non-violent criminal act. The idea of waiting and luring and hiding the crime and the bodies inside the fabric of an average day fits in with the flying-under-the-radar thing.

If Watts is good at flying under the radar, if he's had practise at it [and having an affair with a co-worker and staying off social media also fits in with "under the radar"] then the same can't be said for giving interviews to a phalanx of reporters, or facing a series of interrogations from the FBI, CBI, detectives and cops.

In that last statement Watts reveals an awful lot about his approach in general:

I didn't really talk to people...

I never had a girlfriend in high school...

I was always just like...just flying under the radar.

This why when things went south in his marriage, Watts defaulted in his programming to not talk to anyone about it, perhaps including himself. What I mean is even if he was engaged in an affair, he wasn't really acknowledging either the affair or its implications in a realistic way.

The fact that Watts was not only unsocialized but naïve [in the romantic sense] poured over into his personal life beyond high school and spilled into his marriage.

"He has no game..."

In fact his lack of experience and "game" with the opposite sex may explain why he ended up with Shan'ann, and conversely, why she ended up with him. Neither seemed to choose the other out of a position of strength. Shan'ann was struggling with Lupus and "in a dark place", while Watts had little social cred with the opposite sex or with society in general. Both Shan'ann and Watts seemed to feel misunderstood and maintained few friendships, but Shan'ann clearly outgunned Watts in terms of OCD and her social skills. For one thing she'd been married and divorced, and for another, she was experienced at sales, at pushing people's buttons. Perhaps in terms of their shared OCD [him with cleanliness and orderliness, her with scheduling and regimenting] they felt a sense of mutual understanding and even compatibility.

In a general sense, Watts inability to talk to people goes some way to explaining how he dealt with the conundrum he'd created. Many have asked why Watts didn't simply get divorced. But that would mean confronting and confrontation, and Watts probably felt ill-equipped to spar with Shan'ann. Perhaps he knew he had no game and so, if he played that game openly and honestly [getting divorced] he'd lose. In an odd, twisting inversion of logic, Watts may have reasoned that killing was an easier, safer and quicker solution than talking, and the long term emotional messiness that would invariably follow.

LEE: *Do you feel like you had low self-esteem?*

WATTS [Pregnant pause]: *I wouldn't say low self-esteem. I just didn't want to be part of a group or clique. I had a couple of friends, I sat at the lunch table with 'em. I didn't want a whole lot of friends, just a couple... kinda close-knit. I didn't want to be popular.*

LEE: *Can you attribute that to anything in your childhood; why you...?*

WATTS: *My sister was always the popular one.*

LEE: *Uhuh.*

WATTS: *She was more like my mom...like...more outgoing. Like, me and my grandma would always sit outside waiting for her to come out of middle school, and she would always be the last one out because she had to talk to everybody.*

Watts is playing down the idea of wanting to be popular. This is a mismatch to *The Daily Beast* piece about everyone liking him. He also seemed to be pretty popular or at least well-regarded at work.

Maybe things *were* different in his childhood. Maybe he felt stuck in his sister's shadow, or maybe he *wanted* to be in her shadow, and the shadows in general, because flying under the radar was just easier. But maybe it's deeper and more fraught than that.

There is a sense that all the women in Watts' life are confident and outspoken [including Kessinger], and Watts liked it that way. Watts may have taken his cues from the family unit, including and especially his father. Perhaps he had a sense that to be a man he had to be the strong silent type, and if he wasn't able to be strong he was always able to be silent, and that was seen by the opposite sex as strength and a redeeming quality.

Yet at the same time, Watts clearly gravitated to stronger women [stronger socially, and more confident than himself] who were *not* silent, who could even talk and act on his behalf. Perhaps his mother and his sister did the same on his father's and his behalf, and it was just what he was used to. Perhaps he was used to women wearing the pants, and himself playing second-fiddle.

Perhaps he wanted that with Shan'ann but it got out of hand when Shan'ann got a new lease on life as a Facebook maven. On several occasions Shan'ann is on Facebook saying in how many ways she's changed. Not all of it is a *spiel* to promote Thrive. As she became more outspoken, and pushier on social media the dynamic between the parents deteriorated along with the finances. The Thrive factor had a real impact on both Shan'ann and Watts, making them different, less inhibited but also less down-to-earth than they had once been [including towards one another and towards work, money and family]. The Thrive factor may have made one or both less connected with reality, and more invested in magical thinking [and phantom finances].

As Shan'ann's social cred skyrocketed [on Thrive-fuelled social media at least], her husband's cred as a buff, sexy, ideal husband [the kind of married guy a single woman might find alluring] also peaked, thanks to doubling the dose of Thrive hits.

If Watts felt stuck in Shan'ann's shadow [or caught up in Kessinger's], or maybe he *wanted* to be in Shan'ann's shadow, and under her thumb [until he met Kessinger], he found *some* vestige of confidence or wherewithal to turn the tables on his life. Where did he find it? What reservoir of self-esteem did he use to pick himself up and take his family out? Perhaps he learned somewhere that the way to deal with problems was to *not* deal with them. To duck and dodge, and if necessary, lie. Just keep the ball rolling, keep kicking the can down the road. Let someone else do the heavy lifting.

But then something changed. Watts changed enough to want to affect fundamental change in his life. Murdering his pregnant wife and both daughters was a massive decision, and a massive change to his [and their] circumstances. We get so caught up in how diabolical his crime is, we forget to ponder where Watts found the fuel to commit the crime, the kindling to make it happen. If murder is a cowardly act, the act itself requires a level of twisted courage, but courage all the same. Where'd he get it?

From somewhere else, clearly. Thrive, Kessinger, the work culture at Anadarko, the ego boost that came with a buff new appearance – Watts finally felt man enough to take the bull by the horns and act on his compulsions. Perhaps he found the courage [and the cowardice] in his new self-esteem, which gave him both a new lease on life and a sense of that lease of life being under threat by his wife and children.

We will return to self-esteem later in this narrative. Obviously Watts' denial that self-esteem wasn't a factor doesn't wash. Watts says he was the opposite of his sister; he didn't want to be popular, and:

"I just wanted to be a regular guy..."

His lifestyle and his affair and the murders don't represent anything like that. The fact that he was doing everyone's laundry, his children were belittling him and pelting him with chicken nuggets, his wife was jeering at him occasionally on social media and the cowardly act of the crime itself – all these point to a very weak man, and a man with a very weak sense of self.

The desperate desire to make things work with Kessinger show Watts wanted more, a lot more. A regular guy would have bitten the bullet and gotten divorced. Regular guys don't murder their wives and children.

Page 21 of the *CBI Report* summarises Watts' opinion of rage being a factor in his emotional spectrum:

He cannot recall anything he would have had pent up from child-hood.

A few lines earlier in the report references a Watts who wore braces and wore a Jim Carey bowl haircut. If Watts felt suffocated in a specific sense, and if this shook his sense of self, would he admit it? If he wants so badly to be thought well of, would he really offer up the flaw that he'd spent a lifetime trying to hide from the world?

The rough edges of poverty speak loudly and jarringly into this particular case. When we juxtapose the backstories of both Shan'ann and Watts, when we simply look at the regular jobs and the regular homes of both sets of parents' today, it's difficult to match it to the enormous brown mansion hulking over the other houses in Saratoga Trail. Even the regular folks living in Frederick agreed that the house, inside and out, wasn't a regular house.

"I just wanted to be a regular guy..."

That's bullshit. Regular folks are also regular-sized, and the 245 pound [111 kg] Watts in 2016 was working hard in the summer of 2018 to transform himself into a fitter, leaner 180 pound [81.6 kg] killing machine. It's because he wanted to stand out, not because he wanted to be a regular guy. In fact we could say the psychology driving Watts at school and after school, at work and in his marriage was the opposite:

"I just <u>didn't</u> want to be a regular guy..."

In other words, Watts wanted to escape the circumstances – the rough and irregular deprivations – of childhood. And he worked hard though not always effectively to do that.

When we simply look at the regular jobs Shan'ann held over the years [call-centre nurse, MLM promoter, stay-at-home mom] and Watts' regular job [mechanic, oil worker] the scale and scope of their home, family size, and lifestyle simply don't add up. For a dude with the numeracy skills Watts was supposed to have, the money mess is a massive aberration. So how could two people get so caught up in their own debt bubble not once but twice?

"I just didn't want to be a regular guy..."

When we discover how far the Watts family were living beyond their means, and that <u>they went bankrupt in 2015</u>, we're not shocked. The problem is, Shan'ann and Watts himself don't seem to be shocked either. It hardly features in their messages to one another, or to Shan'ann's pals. It's not a big deal to the Rzuceks or Watts' parents. To date we still don't have Shan'ann's income statements, which may mean the finances aren't a big deal to the investigators either. They weren't to <u>district attorney Michael Rourke during the sentencing hearing</u>, and perhaps they still aren't now.

When Watts is asked about the financial situation [we'll deal with that in detail later], just like the self-esteem dodge, it's no big deal. The only person who seems to see their atrocious financial situation as a big deal precipitating the killings is Kessinger, and it *is* a big fucking deal. If Watts was a wealthier man he could have afforded a divorce. But the poverty without was mirrored by a poverty within.

Harmless Addiction

"The innocence of childhood is like the innocence of a lot of animals." — Clint Eastwood

Having come up with nothing on both the rage and the self-esteem questions, Agent Lee elects to launch an arrow. If he won't offer insights, she'll have a go at triggering some.

LEE: *I know you talked about your dad having an addiction…when I was talking to you…*

WATTS: *That was after I left, left home…*

Agent Lee is trying to get Watts to fess up to *some* childhood trauma somewhere, some source of rage. Watts dodges the dope question by putting it out the childhood spectrum. Yeah his father was a drug addict, but when he was all grown up and wasn't around [so it didn't affect him]. Really?

LEE: *Was it cocaine, or something…?*

WATTS [Still dodging]: *It was some kind of…powder. I'm not sure…*

LEE: *Okay.*

Watts' uncertainty on the substance is hardly credible.

Page 21 of the *CBI Report* refers to Watts' father becoming addicted to "a white powdery substance [possibly cocaine]" after Watts left home. It's hard to believe either the cops or Watts himself can't be more certain or specific about what this "white substance" actually was. But this lack of specificity reveals Watts' loosey-goosey relationship with reality. On a subject as serious as his own father becoming addicted to recreational drugs, Watts is unwilling or unable to nail his colors to the mast. No wonder he himself is unable to do so on criminal matters great and small.

LEE: *How do you think that [his father's addiction] affected you?*

WATTS: *I don't think it affected [interrupts himself]...well...it did affect me but...but, like...it didn't take...like deep down...it didn't really hurt...as much as I thought it would. It was kinda weird. I think it was my mom and my sister told me...*

The *CBI Report* quotes the impact of the father's addiction on the son. Watts' minimizes it.

"It didn't hurt as much as I thought it would."

That sounds like a gambler or someone in debt saying going broke wasn't as tough as he thought it might be.

The critical point, however, is the next one:

When he talked to his father about his addiction, his father immediately changed the subject.

Now for some context...

I was always somebody that tried to coax people down.

Watts talks to his father about his addiction and apparently that's enough to snap his father out of it. Problem solved. Of course, here we also discover something else: the son learning from the father that lying – or fudging – is okay, but besides that, it's a kind of tutorial. See, here's how to deal with tough questions, son – shift the answer away to something else. Here's how to deal with tough things in life, like a marriage on the rocks or a pile of debt, just change the subject. It also reveals a weak father, and that the failure to account for one's sins isn't cowardice but common sense.

I was always just like...just flying under the radar.

I just wanted to be a regular guy...

<u>LEE</u> [Still prodding]: *Did you feel guilty that he started using drugs because you never came home, like he lost his kid...?*

WATTS [Offhand]: *Nah...I never really...knew why he was doin' it...* *

Watts goes on to explain that his mother thought his father was having an affair because "all this money" was disappearing from the house. So here we have a few serious precedents.

1. We have the father lying to his wife.

2. We have a lot of money surreptitiously and systematically disappearing.

3. There's also the notion that his father was having an affair.

Whether he was or not, *the notion itself is normalised* in Watts' mind. The notions of an affair, subterfuge and insurrection within the home as well as the idea of large amounts of money being absconded in secret in service to a mistress all play into a reckless disregard for one's own family. These circumstances, these "sins of the father" played out to a T in the Watts case.

Think about it:

An affair and a critical signal from a credit card purchase that let Shan'ann know something was going on [and something was going on] coincided with the annihilation. Even the drug scenario is in some ways repeated in the excessive and extreme use of Thrive patches.**

Nah...I never really...knew why he was doin' it...

*Watts contradicts himself here. He claims not to know why his father turned to drugs, yet when Lee broaches the subject, Watts immediately provides a reason – that his father turned to drugs to deal with his son leaving home.

**The chemical impact on Watts' homeostasis will be dealt with in more detail. For now it's sufficient to note Watts' use of Thrive patches interfered with his ability to relax and even to sleep. It's possible that by disrupting his sleep Watts' ability to think rationally about what he was doing, and planned to do, was altered in some way, perhaps significantly.

Airport

"Given the circumstances of my childhood, I had the illusion that it's easier to be alone. To have your relationships be casual and also to pose as a solitary person, because it was more romantic. You know, I was raised on the idea of the ramblin' man and the loner." — Steve Martin

On page 22 of the *CBI Report* Watts describes picking his father up from the airport [hours prior to his arrest] and their odd conversations. They discussed sports.

According to the report:

His father always tries to deflect the conversations and change the conversation when they needed to discuss something important.

Of course in order to successfully conduct an affair with Kessinger, which at that moment in time was skidding, and moments from crashing and burning, Watts had had to do all those things. He had to <u>deflect</u> attention away from Shan'ann's pregnancy, and his own Facebook. He had to <u>change</u> conversations, for example during the Sermon on the Porch. An example was when a reporter, *Denver 7's* Tomas Hoppough, asked him if he'd had an emotional conversation with Shan'ann. <u>Watts politely asked the reporter to "leave it at that"</u>.

So the contention that his father couldn't deal with serious issues, coming from Watts, is the pot calling the kettle black. Even so, Ronnie did eventually ask his son if he knew where Shan'ann and the girls were. The report provides Watts' answer verbatim on the final line of text on page 22:

"Maybe he kinda figured out something maybe happened and he just wanted to talk to me as a son."

It's an odd time to do some overdue father-son bonding – the moment you've figured out your kid is suspected of murder. Or perhaps it's the ideal time?

Whatever his father did or didn't do [in terms of white powder, money, addiction and a possible mistress], there were no hard feelings when he found out Watts did what he did. Let's play that again, slowly:

Whatever his father did or didn't do,

there were no hard feelings when he found out Watts did what he did.

That's quite a statement. Imagine if a complete stranger tells you he murdered his neighbor [who was pregnant] and her two daughters. Even if you had zero relationship wouldn't you feel disgust? Wouldn't you feel some sort of natural rancour and resentment? Wouldn't you lash out verbally in some way or demand some kind of explanation?

Now if it was your own flesh and blood wiping out your own flesh and blood, would it still not matter? Would it matter more or less? We know on August 15th, Watts only admitted to murdering Shan'ann, and we also know Shan'ann had personally and directly had a huge falling out with Ronnie and Cindy Watts. We also know the enmity between them and Shan'ann ran back several years, arguably through the course of the marriage from day one. But does it say something – does it say anything – if in-laws don't seem to mind so much if someone they didn't like, someone who wasn't nice to them, was murdered by someone they know? Does it say something – anything – if there is a sense that Shan'ann deserved what happened to her because she was nasty to them, and perceived to be nasty to him?

I think it does say something. If Watts' folks thought Shan'ann's murder was justified for *any* reason, and if they felt it was forgivable, then before the fact wasn't that something Watts could sort of bet on? In other words, while premeditating the murder, didn't he factor into his calculations the utility of Nut Gate, the enmity that had developed* and the certainty that his parents would side with him and support him during the aftermath? In this scenario we imagine Shan'ann and the kids disappearing [permanently] and Watts not getting caught. Would his own parents *mind* if his wife slipped out of existence? Would they need or want an explanation? Would they care?

From Ronnie's perspective, if he had some dirt on his plate, would dirt on his son's tray really be that bad? Would it matter if your own actions as a father were reckless and profligate in comparison** to a son's reckless disregard for life? We must also flip these perspectives. Do they work vice versa?

We have to impute the possibility that when Watts started to entertain the notion of murder [when the premeditation began] it wasn't in a vacuum. The notion of a reckless disregard for family, even if the disregard was only born out of a drug addicted oblivion, *it wasn't alien* to the Watts household prior to the August 13, 2018. Perhaps this better explains Watts' casual and emotionless attitude when describing his inhuman treatment of the lives placed in his care. It wasn't new. He'd been there before.

*Page 728 of the Discovery Documents cites an account of Watts' long-time friend Mark Jamieson, in the aftermath to Nut Gate:

Cindy called him [Jamieson] crying, [following Nut Gate] worried that she had lost [her son] because Shan'ann would turn [her son] against her, as has happened in the past. Jamieson said that is what prompted him to reach out to Watts...Jamieson said that [Watts] initially took Shan'ann's side with the most current fight, but that Cindy then contacted him and told him that [Watts] and Shan'ann were going to separate. [Watts] told Jamieson via text that he had seen the true side of Shan'ann and was done with her.

**Put otherwise: is a criminal in a prison surrounded by criminals more or less accepted by his community compared to a criminal in a church congregation, or a university campus?

Calling Nichol

"A happy childhood has spoiled many a promising life." — Robertson Davies

There's a disorientating discrepancy between the *CBI Report* and the audio when it comes to Kessinger.

Although the conversation happens with less than an hour remaining in the almost five-hours of audio [in the final fifth of the tape in other words], the *CBI Report* deals with Watts talking to Kessinger midway, page 16 of the 31 page report. Then page 24 of the report picks up on the same thread.

Under a section:

With regard to if Watts spoke to Kessinger after the murders…

There is some informal-sounding banter about texting, and which phones he used. At face value, the conversation doesn't seem to mean much or go anywhere. But it's a lead-in to the next section at the bottom of the same page:

With regard to Kessinger being directly or indirectly involved in the murders…

This is one of the lingering questions in the aftermath of a largely unresolved case. Thus, the lead-in is *very* significant. We don't have video footage to examine, so we don't know whether the investigators are sitting with pages of cell phone records in front of them, but it's difficult to believe they either didn't have access to, or knowledge, of these.

It's interesting that none of the three investigators pin Watts down by pulling out a document and asking him to explain a particular call or text. If they ever box him in it's briefly and gently. If he wants to wiggle out, they let him. It's all kept casual and loosey-goosey. If Watts says something they don't seem to understand or agree with, they cycle around it a little, lightly, and then ask him something else. The idea seems to be to stay on his good side, make sure he doesn't get his guard up and no matter what, just keep him talking. Make it seem like he is always getting the benefit of the doubt.

Of course we cannot play those games here.

Page 24 of the report seemingly answers the question about Watts speaking to Kessinger after the murders. The answer is self-evident strictly in the terms the report provides, but the way the report deals with it is surprising.

He spoke to Kessinger on Monday, August 13, 2018.

Yes. We already know that. What did he speak to her about? What did he say? What did she say? The report doesn't specifically say. Unless I've missed it, the audio doesn't seem to have a specific reference to the question either. One would imagine in the report and in the audio that significant time and space would be required to deal with such an important question, and yet there's effectively a single question and a single answer – all of it encapsulated [apparently] in just two lines of text.

Even the information following feels fairly banal and vanilla.

He and Kessinger texted and then spoke on the phone.

Yes. We already know that. What did he speak to her about? What did he say? What did she say? The report doesn't specifically say. We have to go to the audio to get a feel for what's not in the report, and even though it's not dealing directly with what we want to know, we do get some valuable insight *indirectly*.

<u>Are you sure you want to hear this?</u>

LEE: *Was Shan'ann checking your phone...or...?*

WATTS: *She always had my phone.*

LEE: *So how did you get past that?*

WATTS: *I used my work phone.*

LEE: *To text.*

There's no audible response. Watts likely nods here.

LEE: *And you had some secret apps, right?*

WATTS: *That was on my personal phone.*

LEE: *Were you using anything else to have...have contact with her?*

WATTS: *Nah, I just texted her with my work phone, I just...and like uh...when Shan'ann went to North Carolina, I used my personal phone. And she just told me to put pictures in an app, and I just found that calculator...just searched on the...the apps store...like hidden pictures.*

LEE: *So your iCloud wasn't linked together, so she wouldn't know if you were getting apps...*

WATTS: *It used to be...a long time ago. But uh...when we got different phones, for uh...when our phone contact list would be synced up in the cloud, stuff like that...I couldn't handle it. She had like tons-tons of phone contacts. But it still kinda linked up at one point.*

The above script is worth reading and listening to more than once. Lee starts off asking Watts about how he communicated with Kessinger. Only one line of text in the report deals with this, but we're going to spend more time on it than that; flesh it out some.

The first insight is that Shan'ann always had Watts' phone. In a global sense, that's a massive invasion of privacy and, in a scenario like that, the walls are already pretty tight for a husband bent on pursuing an affair while his wife is pregnant.

Basically, Shan'ann's surveillance of her husband amounted to hypervigilance – not just about money [what he was bringing in each month, how much he was spending and on what] – but also his communication. Shan'ann also had the use of and access to his Facebook.

But the nugget *Rocket Science* wants to hold up to the light is the fact that in spite of Shan'ann's exceptional access, Watts hid his communication [the affair, the texts, the nude photos] in plain sight. Even though he knew she was going to look through his phone when he met her in North Carolina, and during their two days together before she headed to Phoenix on business, he brazenly had everything on his personal phone, just hidden behind a harmless looking app. No lightning bolts there. The lightning bolt is how this sly and sneaky psychology matches up with Watts hiding his crime in the rudiments of getting up and going to work. This can't be overstated.

I was always just like…just flying under the radar.

The way Lee asks him about his phone and the way he sneakily responds, implying that he simply switched phones to avoid detection, doesn't answer the full portent of the question. Not even close. And this is what Watts has been doing all along. Providing little morsels of compromising truth while holding the fort, and keeping the big, putrid fruitcake in a dungeon behind a psychological lock and key. Watts is happy to banter all day in the courtyard, in front of the castle, throwing crumbs to the crows. What his interrogators want is the key to that dungeon. He's not giving it, and they're not getting it as long as they place nice.

But we don't have to.

What does Watts mean when he says:

"And she just told me to put pictures in an app, and I just found that calculator…just searched on the…the apps store…like hidden pictures."

Who is he talking about when he says "she told me"? Who else could it be but Kessinger? Kessinger was sending him compromising pictures of herself. Why would Shan'ann tell him where to put pictures on his phone? Once again, it's telling that the investigators don't hit the pause button here and deal with this. The audio is so bad, it's difficult to tell where [or whether] the sound is edited out or not, and perhaps that's intentional. Perhaps white noise was edited in after the fact.

If Kessinger helped Watts conceal her nude selfies on his phone – from Shan'ann – that hardly makes her guilty of a much larger crime. But it does start to unlock the door of two people conspiring together. Obviously every affair in the history of the world involves two people conspiring. By affair we mean two consenting adults engaging in an illicit romance while both of them are fully aware that at least one of them is married. In a situation like that, a conspiracy is inevitable.

The other aspect we want to hover over is this business of the iCloud. Watts isn't known for his verbosity, and yet on the iCloud question he has a lot to say. They were linked, then they weren't. Then they were again. In this extended game world of spying and sneaking and subterfuge, it's not just the straying husband that must cover his tracks, he must also spy on his wife to spot opportunities and anticipate movements. Potentially the iCloud offered Watts even better access to Shan'ann's world than she to his [via using his phone and his derelict social media.] If this is true, then Watts potentially saw the debate as it began – about his wife's awareness of the affair and her response, and the response of Nickole Atkinson and Cassie Rosenberg.

Even within the confines of the guilty adulterer, Watts – assuming he saw the vitriol between the three women – would have felt deeply betrayed. If he had innocently strayed from Shan'ann [if such a word can even be associated with adultery] then *her* rage and *her* response would feel sickeningly malevolent. Take his house, take his children, fuck you, fuck you and fuck you. Shan'ann never used those words in that way, but Watts said she did during his false confession to his father [implicating her in the murders of the children]. Didn't Watts do that because he'd seen all the fuck yous from her [behind his back] in the iCloud? It sure feels that way, doesn't it?

Is there anything else to go on? There might be. Remember page 728 of the Discovery Documents, when Watt's pal Mark Jamieson told the cops:

[Watts] initially took Shan'ann's side with the most current fight, but that Cindy then contacted him and told him that [Watts] and Shan'ann were going to separate. [Watts] told Jamieson via text that he had seen the true side of Shan'ann and was done with her.

Watts may have been less than honest about his feelings, but perhaps the emotional reality here is louder and more authentic than we've realized. Nut Gate was a sort of the opening act to the next phase of Shan'ann's response to the catastrophe unfolding around her. The "true side" Watts saw, the side that was like a dagger into his own heart, was what she said not *to* him but *about* him. Wasn't that it? Wasn't *that* the license, the excuse he used to do away not only with her but with the kids, because if he lost he'd lose it all, including the kids and the house? And if he needed a push to do what he was already tempted to do, the push didn't just come from Kessinger, it came from Shan'ann.* The source of his rage, arguably, was *her rage*, as well as the fear of confronting it one on one, man to woman.

I was always just like...just flying under the radar.

I just wanted to be a regular guy...

---

*In fairness to Shan'ann, all of us have said very mean things and expressed hateful intentions to others. That is very different from expressing them directly to that person. Firstly, if one elects not to express these sentiments it means one harbors love and hope and the venting and ranting was just that. Secondly, if one does express these sentiments, it offers a right of response. The great failure in this case is that Watts took this right away from Shan'ann [and the children, and his unborn child]. In this context, he may have felt justified in his mutiny. His right of response had been suppressed for months, for years, and this – the murders – was his way of getting his life back. The whole point was that their lives no longer be at his expense. If this is how Watts justified his motives to himself, they nevertheless don't wash in society, and he knew it. For this reason the crime remains hidden and the why undisclosed. Watts' knows why but he also knows it's an *unacceptable why* to everyone besides himself.

Mental Patient

"The worst loneliness is to not be comfortable with yourself." — Mark Twain

Page 26 of the *CBI Report* references Watts' mental health. This is another gaping hole in the evidence file. While we can speculate until the cows come home, it would be hugely instructive if Watts submitted to a proper battery of personality, psychology and mental health screenings.

It's obvious Watts *was* subjected to exhaustive tests of *some* kind while at the Denver Reception and Diagnostic Center. According to Watts he had his IQ tested, though it seems weird and scarcely believable that eleven separate tests were needed to figure out his IQ, and even less plausible that someone who sold his car for less than he owed on it [and whose wife wouldn't allow him to touch their finances*] could muster a triple digit IQ, let alone in the 130s or even higher.

Perhaps Watts is very bright in some areas [numeracy but not financial accounting] but exceedingly daft in others [social settings and common sense]. Watts' execution of the crime is impressively smart from a purely true crime perspective. He hides the crime within the fabric of a ~~day~~ workday morning, and that part at least is almost flawless. He left virtually no evidence traces in the home, and had he not caved and provided the exact location of the bodies, one wonders how long it would have taken to recover them.

But there are other aspects that don't bring to mind a prodigy. The MLM circus that is so idiosyncratic to the Watts case hardly seems to be the stuff of genius. The ham acting in the videos wasn't so different from Watts' ham acting to the cops and in front of television cameras. His explanation for what happened to Shan'ann was badly conveyed, and by leaving her smartphone at home suggested he'd overanalysed the crime itself, but forgotten to think much about the aftermath, or the difficult questions that would invariably follow.

The smart/stupid debate is a very black and white debate at any rate. Whether he's a genius or a moron, it still doesn't explain the driving psychology, the operant psychology or the family dynamics at work. It doesn't explain why.

The aspect that does explain this area, one that we have not spent much time on during the first seven narratives, is the psychology and mental health of the extended families [Shan'ann, her younger brother and her parents as one family unit and Watts, his much older sister and his parents as the other].

We don't need to be Freud or Jung, and we don't need a battery of psyche tests to figure out the basic psychology of the Rzuceks from Aberdeen or the Wattses down the road in Spring Lake. What we see from a distance is a strange mismatch between the relatively calm and collected Rzuceks and their highly strung-daughter. In many ways Watts seems a lot like his father-in-law; gentle, sweet, good-natured, quiet, deferring to his somewhat overbearing wife. That's not to cast stones at Sandi, even Shan'ann herself didn't always want to talk to her mother, and when the Rzuceks moved into Saratoga Trail for 16 months, the stress levels went through the roof as Sandi instructed her daughter on how to raise Bella and Celeste. Watts also mentions that it was never a good idea to wake Sandi too early in the morning.

But while the Rzuceks had ample reason to hold a grudge during the sentencing hearing, they didn't. There's been some barbed rancour from Frankie Junior, especially on social media, but overall, the Rzuceks seem relaxed and congenial people.

In the context of her family, certainly her parents, Shan'ann *feels* like the odd one out. We know the Rzuceks were all too familiar with Shan'ann's moods and temper, which is why when Watts let them know [shortly after the disappearance on Monday] that Shan'ann was in "one of her moods"** it made sense *then and there*. It took someone really close to Shan'ann*** to fathom that her disappearance had nothing to do with her moodiness even though she was very distressed [about the charge to credit card, the likelihood of an affair, Watts' attitude to the third pregnancy, the marital uncertainty etc.].

If Shan'ann was prickly and high maintenance, she was still close to her family. Watts wasn't. Probably in some ways, perhaps the most significant, his own family were to blame for allowing a distance to intrude. If they held grudges, well, they held them for years.**** This is really the crux of the matter, because when family hold grudges, essentially what they're saying is:

I'm done. You're dead to me.

Obviously it's not murder, and it's not a literal death. It's a symbolic cutting of social ties. It can be just as painful as real death, however, because there's a prolonged physical absence and a prolonged purposeful neglect. We see this fulminating on the Spring Lake side of things against Shan'ann, and perhaps leaking over into their son's life, where

Watts lost his close relationship with his father and to some extent the rest of his family too. Shan'ann's bristling personality had something to do with that [as we saw during Nut Gate], but Watts' parents weren't blameless either.

Rather than taking anyone's side, we ought to look at the damaging impact of holding grudges within families and how it played out in this case. The grudges that flared up during Nut Gate were ugly and nasty, and while many have gotten caught up choosing sides and figuring out how nut allergies in children work, we lose sight of how this explosion must have looked and felt to Watts from the perspective of Colorado, and his mistresses' bed.

Let's try to sit quietly on that idea for a few moments. On the one hand, Watts may have sided with Shan'ann reflexively, simply because of the reality that the health of one of his children had [theoretically] been placed in jeopardy.

An article in the _Daily Mail_ summarising this incident***** puts it in a strange, otherworldly perspective:

Prior to her death, Watts said that his wife Shan'ann believed that her in-laws were trying to kill her daughter, who had a nut allergy, by serving nuts near her…

When we spend a little time with that statement it starts to feel odd, then ridiculous. Really? The grandparents were trying to kill, to murder Ceecee? And yet when one goes through the correspondence, it's hard to make the case that that's not what Shan'ann was saying. She rails about protecting her children, and how evil the grandmother is and how stupid the grandfather. Further, she warns Watts if he doesn't stand up to them [and support her, and support their children], then he is with them, and guilty as well.

It's tempting to get caught up in the emotion, and to lose track of Watts half-watching this unfold and half-ignoring it from the safety of Colorado, and his mistresses embrace. We can see that if Watts initially went along with the rollercoaster, at some point he had a change of heart and got off the rollercoaster.

...his wife Shan'ann believed that her in-laws were trying to kill her daughter...

What Shan'ann was effectively doing by demonstrating the cutting of all her bonds with the Watts family [and even him if he didn't find his balls], was that if *she* felt justified she could do the worst possible thing. The strange dynamic that then emerges is a festering of grudges online, where Facebook relationships are rescinded. We've all been there and felt the sting when someone close to us finally blocks us, even when this is deserved. It's a virtual act, but the symbolism behind it is very real. Even when it's us pressing the button, and the object of our disaffection isn't even in the room, the burning pain in one's chest is real. Social death is almost as powerful and often as real as actual death. And so *this* presaged the actual deaths. This was the psychological preparation that prepared the soil for the seeds of triple murder.

The other aspect to look at is a scenario where Watts is playing with the possibility of Ceecee *actually* dying from an allergic reaction. He's simply playing it out and seeing how it plays. When the magic line was crossed where an idea becomes an intention [all within the premeditation phase] he continues to imagine them no longer being there, and though he has some triggers of resistance, the wolves of reinforcement howl louder. It may be that from his mistresses' bed he was surprised *not to mind* the idea of never seeing the younger, and sicklier child. This errant impulse then joined hands with the feeling of resistance that he simply didn't want the third child. And that he was dreading the return of his wife. And if he did something he wasn't supposed to when Shan'ann wasn't around, but the kids were, Bella would tell on him.******

While Shan'ann was sort of crying wolf, Watts was actually playing with the idea in his mind of extinguishing lives. What might that feel like – for him. What would that achieve except instant relief – for him. But how could he go about it? Might he even…get away with it? In the previous chapter we've examined the notion that access to the iCloud was the last push Watts needed for the gritty, metallic resolve that lands on the tongue when a murder is genuinely on the cards.

In those vitriolic messages he saw the grudges extended to him too, and would rip his home from under his feet, and along with them, his children. And because Watts was both ensconced in a relationship that pleased him and completely and utterly outgunned online and in the real world [remember Shan'ann was already in North Carolina blowing up his ancestral home and turning his children – maybe – against him], so he knew he was completely out of the game. If he took Shan'ann on he would lose, but a mêlée – thanks to the pregnancy – was looking inevitable. The only way to fight [as he saw it] and win was to fight fire with water. He had to fight or he'd lose everything. But if he fought it was all or nothing. To give his all meant reducing them to nothing [yes, even his children], but at least he'd come out the other side with a house, a woman who loved him and who could bare him healthy children, and a family who was no longer behind a barrier erected by his rampaging wife.

As unpleasant as this is to stomach, it reveals to us how certain members of the Watts family were extinguished *symbolically* in a late skirmish, but by no means an isolated one. And so, this symbolic extermination of close family members – purposefully and permanently

– provided the psychological handholds for Watts to contemplate the unthinkable.

Whether we feel contempt for Watts' motives or not, we ought to take fair warning from it. By holding and maintaining grudges in our own lives, especially against family members and/or people we supposedly loved once upon a time, we open the doors in our own hearts to evil. A grudge [the internal, symbolic killing of someone else while they are still alive, by pretending they do not matter, and do not exist] is a precursor to something worse. And whether the something worse happens or not, the result of a grudge is the same: whoever puts the grudge in place places *himself* behind bars. A grudge is a prison not for someone else, but for you.

*Ever since he sold his 4-wheeler for less than what he owed on it, Shan'ann wouldn't let him do anything with their finances. [CBI Report, page 17].

**Discovery Documents, page 679 makes one of three references to "moods". The others are on page 696 [Kessinger describing Watts' mood which had changed regarding purchasing an apartment] and page 1432, where Frank tells the cops Watts told Sandi disappeared during "one of her moods".

***Nickole Atkinson was keenly aware of Shan'ann's medical situation and doctor's appointment, which is why she also knew it made no sense that she'd leave her car and phone [her lifeline] at home and just disappear. In this simple sense Atkinson was a lot smarter at joining the dots than Watts was at rubbing a few out.

****Neither of Watts' parents – nor his sister Jamie – attended his wedding. The message behind a grudge – effectively – is that it nullifies a person. Thus, the message behind the boycott of the wedding, and to some extent the marriage as a whole, was to nullify it [Shan'ann and by extension, the children that were borne out of it.] This provided Watts with a psychological and symbolic license to do the same thing. The Watts Family Murders were a manifestation of a longstanding indictment of his wife by her parents-in-law, executed by the son, and extended to his own children. The affair and Nut Gate activated this psychology opportunistically, which is to say the grudges provide a convenient scapegoat for rationalizing triple murder.

*****The same *Daily Mail* article refers specifically to mental health issues at play within the Watts saga. Citing the *CBI Report*, the *Mail* notes:

[Watts] said that his parents, Cindy and Ronnie Watts, encouraged him [to] argue he was a victim of emotional and mental abuse [referring to how they perceived Shan'ann's treatment of them, and him] when the case went to trial...

******When Ronnie Watts wanted to FaceTime with his granddaughters at 14:33 on August 10th [Shan'ann had just left for Phoenix], even though the coast was clear, father and son decided between themselves that it simply wasn't worth "getting anything started". His father's assessment then basically sums up the kind of stranglehold Shan'ann could have on others close to her, even when she was far away:

"If she finds out she would probably have a fit."[Discovery Documents, page 2111].

MONEY

"The man who does not value himself, cannot value anything or anyone." — Ayn Rand, *The Virtue of Selfishness: A New Concept of Egoism*

Enter the Colosseum

"It was driving me crazy that I couldn't remember something that I studied the night before. All it did was trigger my anxiety, and all of sudden everything would snowball on me." —Terry Bradshaw

I f the driving force for this case can be reduced to a single word it's greed, but the *emotion* driving that greed is fear, and above all, *fear fuelled by inadequacy.* Inadequacy [which is lack, shortage, meagreness, scantiness] can't be undone with excess.

Fear lurks in the lives of all four of the original members of the Watts family. Shan'ann had a fear for most of her life about a disease that could flare up without warning and consume her from within.* She also had a fear that she wouldn't be able to conceive children, or that they would inherit her sickness. The children by some accounts *were* sickly. Page 17 of the *CBI Report* notes:

They had a lot of doctor bills from <u>the girls always being sick</u>.

Celeste had a fear of being imperilled if she ate nuts. This fear was such a clear and present danger, <u>Bella's sleep was disturbed</u> as late as the night [August 11th] prior to her murder [on August 12th]. Bella was worried that if Celeste went to sleep she might not wake up, and thus, if

Bella went to sleep, she might wake up with her sister gone. Tragically, this fear was not unfounded.

For Watts the fear was being found out about the affair, *but as an introvert* his fear of being found out by Shan'ann going into full melt-down was magnified; it was more akin to *terror* than fear. This is what makes the *spiel* of Watts simply confessing the affair** to Shan'ann so ridiculous. Those who believe it simply have no understanding of the dynamic between Watts and his wife, as well as the levels of anxiety – not stress, anxiety – these people were facing day to day as individuals and as a group.

The cavity of inadequacy can't be filled with stuff. It's a hole from childhood that can't be filled by a big house or an expensive car. It can only be fixed from the inside, or not at all.

That's a nice little paragraph, but human history is awash with the blood and guts of men who have ruined and wrecked their lives by trying to fix themselves from the outside. Money is a default device to do that. Ask the average person what they wish for most, it's to win the lottery. Money will keep the wolves at bay. Money is the key to the fairy tale, right?

Like it or not, money and self-esteem go together like a sock into a shoe, or a hand into a glove. To understand the interplay between money and self-esteem we have to spend some time opening the rusty tin can that is self-esteem. What do the worms inside *taste* like, exactly? Sometimes they taste like chopped liver.

Now, to understand how deeply rooted self-esteem and chopped liver are in a mythic and totemic sense, we need to dive into reality, and dwell in the swirling dusts of ancient history. Disoriented? Good. You're about to feel winds on your upper lip, and dust billowing against your sleeves and trouser legs.

Mind open? Imagination and Visualisation switch set to ON?

Taking a break from the Watts case, I spent 27 days in May 2019 travelling through Europe. One of my stops was <u>Arles</u>, a small city in present-day southern France that was once of considerable importance in the Roman province of <u>Provincia Nostra</u>. Arles is a community about 2000 years old, so yes, older than most.

<u>I visited the colosseum in Arles</u>, and was interested to discover <u>the circular ruins once held an entire village inside</u>. Over time the colosseum in Arles filled with houses and its circular walls served as a kind of barrier. Then the village fell into ruin and was excised, and <u>today we see the colosseum as if the village never existed</u>. Today it's a tourist attraction and the lives it held [as a village] are all but forgotten. Well, what about the lives lost *purposely* within its walls – by design in fact – to rapturous applause?

Ernest Becker references the times that birthed the colosseum in *The Structure of Evil*. Bear with me, this is important. Becker focuses on Imperial Rome's intentions to institutionalize [to reduce a community to a formal system] a society built on slavery and private gain. The world we know today with all its institutions and systems, evolved from the Roman model. What was that model exactly? Well, Becker tells us. It was:

"...sustained by domination; [Imperial Rome] was devoted to individual glory..."

Becker describes the inauguration of the original colosseum [in Rome]. It involved killing 5000 animals in the first month. He adds:

"As one reads Roman history it seems that the endless portrait heads of favored citizens, which stuff our museums, were paid for in the blood of proud lions and equally courageous men...They were after what higher

primates need most, a sense of self-value, one that is constructed out of symbolic acts, in place of one built by neural circuits..."

Becker concludes by comparing the modern world to the "potlatch" of the colosseum.

"[Capitalism and materialism] fails because man's basic sense of self-value can only be had by doing, and not by merely owning..."

All of that is a roundabout way of saying the reduction of heroes and lions to pieces of gushing chopped liver on a dusty substrate in some Roman province or prefecture, makes those watching feel good about themselves. They are voyeurs in the symbolic battles playing out below the soles of their feet. When those they side with [man or lion] win, they do too, or it *feels* that way. Of course in reality, it's only a sense of one gaining *a sensation of power* at another's expense.

We ought to see this transaction of blood and dust, life and death, applause and death, in the *schema* of the Thrive *spiel*. So we float 2000 years forward in time from the dust of a Roman province to the dust of Colorado. Owning Thrive patches and owning cars and having a particular lifestyle are enthusiastically promoted and applauded all day, every day. And while this is happening, while champions are raised and praised on social media, the losers flush away their last savings and withdraw into ignominy and insignificance. Same deal, different day, just far bigger colosseums and cauldrons filled with gold.

Becker describes the Romans bolstering their private potlatch with public bread and circuses.

"They outdid themselves to divert the dispossessed masses and to earn glory by the most conspicuous consumption..."

Presumably by consumption in the context of the colosseum he means the consumption of actual lives, through slaughter. It may seem excessive to compare MLM companies to this, or the damage done by fracking operations to *terra firma* and the fabric of society, but the Watts Family Murders are simply a literal interpretation of all these impulses and analogies.

Watts murders in order to win a home, a mistress and a new life for himself. The gladiators did the same to wild applause. MLM murders the truth in pursuit of a private fairy tale. It's the same thing over and over again – chopped liver in exchange for self-esteem. Sometimes the transaction involves people killing other people, or animals, or eco-systems. Sometimes it involves a husband or wife turning their spouse into a doormat.

Now let's get practical.

*Lupus was a reality in the final week of Shan'ann's life. On August 5th, Shan'ann sent Watts this text bristling with pique:

*I'm not kidding Christopher. I'm having a bad experience these last few days with my pregnancy and **I'm spotting**. I'm not dealing with it...*

The spotting reference may be an informal term for systemic lupus erythematosus.

**It's interesting that Watts seemed to have no qualms letting his father know about the affair, and the affair didn't seem a big deal to Ronnie [or Cindy for that matter] when he found out. When *did* Ronnie find out? It must predate their reunion in the interrogation room in mid-August. And yet Watts initially denied the affair when asked directly by the cops, he denied it again when asked by Coder and a third time during the polygraph. By then of course, Kessinger had already informed the FBI that she'd been "actively involved" in an affair right up to the morning of the disappearance. These words – actively involved – appear in the arrest affidavit. When Watts was confronted with the affair – Coder told him they knew who she was, and mentioned Kessinger by name – Watts admitted cryptically the affair was the only thing he was holding back [Discovery Documents, page 600]. His initial reaction to the affair and how it related to the disappearance of his family was to say he couldn't bring himself to tell Shan'ann [Discovery Documents, page 601]. This is the applicable reference:

Coder asked [Watts] if [there] was a misunderstanding and [Watts] said the only misunderstanding was that he didn't tell Shan'ann about the affair. [Watts] said he couldn't bring himself to tell Shan'ann about the affair.

On page 602, obviously moving through a lot of actual interrogation, Watts adapts his stance and has Shan'ann ask him about the affair.

...he talked to Shan'ann about the separation, the house, and Shan'ann asked about the affair. [Watts] said Shan'ann had mascara running down her face and it was very emotional.

On page 603 Watts takes it slightly further:

*[Watts] said he knew Shan'ann knew in her heart about his affair, but **she was waiting for him to admit it**. [Watts] said he believed **Shan'ann just lost it** because **she knew he was cheating and he denied it**. Ronnie asked [Watts] if that was the point Shan'ann went off [but] Watts said [that] was when Shan'ann started crying.*

In this version Shan'ann doesn't lash out, she simply weeps in resignation.

During the Sermon on the Porch, when Watts was asked about the conversation, and whether it was an argument, <u>Watts said</u>:

"It wasn't like an argument [swaying, glances up at the ceiling]. We had an emotional conversation [smiles]. But...I'll leave it at that...but...it's...[smiles openly]..."

It should also be noted in both Watts' versions the affair plays a *casual role* in the discussion leading up to Shan'ann's murder. In the first version [the confession in August, the First Confession], it's simply broached, along with the idea of selling the house, but there's no immediate reaction. Later, when he's out of the bedroom, it seems to activate Shan'ann, leading her to murder her own children. In the second version [the confession in February, the Second Confession], Shan'ann confronts him about an affair but he denies it. After having sex he tells her he doesn't love her, and then strangles her. The problem with both these versions are that, in terms of how the affair plays into the dynamics, they're both *too casual* and thus unrealistic, and therefore untrue.

Self-Esteem and Chopped Liver

"People should know when they are conquered."
— <u>Quintus</u>, *Gladiator [2000]*

D espite his denial in Dodge, self-esteem was a factor in this case. As <u>was recently commented on the *CrimeRocket* page</u>, "Chris had done everything right…" In the marriage, as a father and provider, that was mostly true. Of course, the affair was a major departure from that. It was really out of character for Watts, but that's the point. Who he was, or who he had become, was changing. As Simba's father in The Lion King intones:

"<u>You are more than what you have become…</u>"

Watts and his wife both felt that way but in very different ways. The money, or the agonising lack of it, manifested in both their lives in very much the same way, however.

We all know the feeling where we feel like we're owed something, that we deserve more. Well, in Kessinger's company, that feeling felt ecstatically but alarmingly real, and if he didn't grasp it, he might lose it forever.

If Shan'ann was happily married, or at least *invested* enough in her marriage and her role as a mother to want it to continue, Watts wasn't. He's somewhat wishy washy on this score at times, occasionally giving his marriage a clean bill of health, while at other times being more authentic about his feelings and the true vibe behind closed doors.

In the Discovery Documents, Coder asks Watts at one point:

Why couldn't you be yourself around your wife?

Watts replies:

I just felt like I'd always have to change who I was. Because I'm - I was always about - I mean I was doing the lau- I'd be - I do everything...

The above is a verbatim quote from the discovery. The stuttering is transcribed as it's stated. Why is there so much stress around such a simple question? For one thing we can see Watts resented having to do the laundry for everyone. In a scenario where one person is *very* OCD, very regimented, very controlling, very dominant [we can argue how much constitutes "very" or what OCD actually is, or we can accept that whatever it is, it was excessive to Watts], and the other person is, as Shan'ann put it, chopped liver, introverted, pliant, then we can see how one person can start to walk all over the other.

Shan'ann was attracted to Watts *because* he was chopped liver. He was no threat to her simply because he wasn't domineering. He was a quiet, dutiful, nice guy. After her divorce Shan'ann wanted someone more compliant. When Watts let her lie on his lap for several hours, it wasn't his appearance or his character or his affection or attention to her that won her heart, it was his meek compliance.

The Urban Dictionary definition of chopped liver is:

Someone perceived as being of little value or worth, as evidenced by being ignored when others are getting attention.

Within those terms, Shan'ann's description implicitly acknowledges two things:

1. She thinks he's chopped liver.

2. He thinks he's chopped liver.

But it also implies that she knows *he* knows he's chopped liver, and *he* knows she knows he knows he's chopped liver. Does that make sense? It's one thing to be chopped liver, it's another to have someone else hold that over you and sort of make it into *their* mantra. In the Colosseum sense, it's one thing to encounter a lion in your life, it's another to have someone manufacture the encounter, and make it into their entertainment. In the same way, it's one thing to make attempts as a merchant selling one's wares, it's another to be a pawn in the scheme of a cynical corporate, where the profits are not to be made from products per se, but by turning the players [the gladiators/promotors] into buckets of blood and gold.

If Watts was resigned to be chopped liver, then there were a few things to look forward to. A home of his own, for starters. A pay check that, in spite of his shortcomings, could buy him building blocks of self-esteem. But none of that is of any reassurance when he discovers he's simply chopped liver in someone else's Colosseum, and his money [his blood] isn't of any worth other than for it to be seen to be spilled [at his expense].

Shan'ann was attracted to Watts *because* he was chopped liver. Which is why Shan'ann was *expecting* Watts to dance to her tune even when she annihilated his parents. Just because he'd always done it, it was his duty to do what he was told, but this was ultimately a bridge too far. His self-esteem, such as it was, wouldn't permit it. Shan'ann was used to getting her way, pushing, controlling, promoting. Even if she was justified in blasting Cindy, expecting her son to turn against his mother and father on her command in this context [let alone *any* context] is crossing a serious line.

The notion of a person being chopped liver absolutely goes hand in hand with notions of self-esteem. Whether it's you who is Chopped Liver or someone else who has to deal with chopped liver, self-esteem is definitely going to come into play, probably as some sort of tug-of-war for power.

In Chopped Liver's case, the war will be about how little power he gets over his piece of his little world. In the other person's case, for examples the Romans of the Colosseum, it will be how much power they get to enjoy over Chopped Liver. The more liver that gets chopped, the more entertaining and the more they feel like gods of this Earth.

Do you see? The one's rise seems to go hand in hand with the other's fall, meaning: as one spouse becomes more and more domineering, the other has be increasingly submissive and self-deprecating to keep the peace.

I want to emphasize that the transactionality we observe here is unavoidable. Transactionality is inescapable. What true crime tries to establish is the degree of it. Because there's the happy transactionality in the give and take of happy marriage, or a harmonious, beneficial business operation [such as a farm producing sustainable crops of organic vegetables]. We live in a world, however, that doesn't seem to object to the kind of transactionality that is so permissive, it's criminal. This is why we treat celebrities and the uber-rich as heroes.

I want to idle for a moment on transactionality, just so we can understand its nuts and bolts and the whole machinery.

Becker refers to all organisms that necessarily experience "self-feeling", that is, an individual experience of being alive. Sounds simple, but he takes it further. This "self-feeling" derives from organisms transacting with other objects.

"...organisms need other objects to come into being...We talk about high self-esteem and low self-esteem according to someone's ability to navigate satisfactorily in his cultural world. Man tends to feel good about himself when he can address himself to a dependable range of objects for his satisfactions, and when he has a firm command of the rules or behaviours..."

Becker adds that a man is necessarily composed of an amalgam of the objects with which he transacts, so that a man's personality is effectively self-feeling, objects and rules [or behaviours]. Watts was "transacting" with a sexual object. Her rules were becoming his, her self-feeling his [and vice versa].

Shan'ann, meanwhile, was transacting in a very symbolic environment, forming virtual relationships and selling, in a sense, virtual products [powders, patches, self-esteem]. Shan'ann's power and leadership in this area meant she felt she could wield and withdraw these magical energies at will. But magic thinking only takes you so far.

All things being equal, even if Watts remained faithful to Shan'ann, it's difficult to believe they would have held on to their house – and lifestyle – for much longer, even if they'd stayed married. And as the losses piled up, one wonders how long either spouse would have put up with the other. It's hard to imagine that with their world crumbling they themselves wouldn't collapse like card houses too. If they insisted, perhaps they could sell, move back and move in with the Rzuceks for 16 months [wouldn't that be fun for the son-in-law] until the haemorrhage was sorted. But this would likely involve Watts losing his job in Colorado and Shan'ann having to make a serious life choice, steering her away from the only career she really knew through and through – MLM. Could she do that? Would she?

We know what happened though, Watts did cheat on Shan'ann, but the cheating didn't just happen randomly. He had to be pretty miserable to stray in the first place, and once embroiled in the affair, he had to be desperate about avoiding a reset back to married life with kids, given the lengths he went to. Again, we're not condoning the crime, we're simply acknowledging the emotional currents that were flowing within the family dynamic prior to the annihilation.

In the Second Confession, Watts doesn't seem authentic when he talks about his conversation with Kessinger about whether he was happily married.

WATTS: *If I'd never met Nikki would I have ever, you know, thought... our relationship...was...bad? Nikki said, 'I don't want you to leave your wife just because of me.' I said, 'What do you mean?' She said, 'If you hadn't met me would you have known, like...' Cos I'd never thought I would have strayed away from her at all. Like I've never tried to...like... follow anybody.*

It's a nice gesture from Watts to let Kessinger off the hook. But it's not what he does during his first go round, with Coder in particular. Watts was clearly still smitten by Kessinger during those early interrogations, so much so Coder had to remind Watts to focus on his family, and to talk about *them*.

So, where does all of this take us to at the end of the day? We see that Watts clearly felt justified in the affair, in the sense that he wanted to protect the affair, and was intent on destroying his family to make that happen. But more than that, he likely felt justified *in himself* as Shan'ann's behaviour became increasingly narcissistic and antisocial. If there had been no Nut Gate, and no vehemence to his parents in those final few weeks, would Watts still have done what he did? It's difficult to say. Perhaps the finances were a more powerful driving force.

Of course the venom, vehemence and vitriol coming in a series of explosions from North Carolina, tied to perilous finances and a possible eavesdropping of enraged outbursts on iCloud, all these could have sparked memories of a long and troubled marriage, and stoked coals that were already heated by sex and a thirst for mistress-cash.

But a single ingredient could have neutralized all sparks, and contained the damage of all explosions. A single ingredient would have kept his coals cool no matter how much they were stoked. Self-esteem.

If his inner world was stable and secure, and there was a sense of sufficiency, there would be no need to do anything, or change anything. But in spite of appearances, Watts' inner world *was* in turmoil – *everything* was unstable and insecure. He felt a sense of insufficiency in terms of his own family, even in terms of a home he was paying for, or thought he was. So his self-esteem *was* being eroded.

What makes this case so unusual, and the criminal so unfathomable, is that there's also a contradiction right here. Just as his self-esteem was being chipped away in one dimension, it was also being built up and recast in another [hence *TWO FACE*].

This recasting was making him into a new man, as it were. He was starting to dream of another life with her. He was starting to do things he never did with Shan'ann, like go camping, watch movies, dine out, have a lot of sex. He was starting to think of his childhood fondly, along with his father's joyful participation in it. He was starting to calibrate his finances, and how deep the malaise went.

Kessinger was a big part of his transformation, so was Thrive – and his work-culture perhaps played a larger role in the recasting than we imagine.

It feels mean and downright nasty to use words like narcissistic and antisocial to describe Shan'ann, especially when the same words describe Watts. The point is they were mirrors of one another. He was narcissistic in his affair, she on Facebook and perhaps in her love of emotional excess and indulgence. We're not saying they're equal in their narcissism, simply reflections.

He was antisocial in terms of the crime he committed, she in her grudges and attacks on his family. It feels like victim blaming, but it likely is exactly how Watts felt about her before annihilating his family. He had to blame her for something. And her increasing, unbridled narcissism [as he saw it] was becoming intolerable. Remember, it's not her narcissism in a vacuum, or his in a vacuum, it's hers and his rubbing one another the wrong way. Narcissism tends to do that. Our own narcissism never bothers us, and it's hardly noticeable. But it's what bothers others the most about us. In social media terms, we may love our own numbers when it comes to the attention we get, but despise those of others, especially those more popular than we are. This is normal narcissism simply doing its natural gyrations to the beat of our egos.

So what we want to focus on when we deal with these difficult questions is relate them to both Shan'ann and Watts. We don't want to take sides, or from the outset proclaim how justified anyone was in what they did. We simply want to understand why, and *how* the why came to be. Once we know the why on its own merits, then we can turn it into a piñata. Make sense? But first we have to figure out the why without fear or favor.

"I didn't have access to the bank account..."

"It was like I was walking just like I-I got, you know, like, walk on eggshells type of thing. It's kind of like you don't - you f-feel like you're always doing something that's wrong." — Chris Watts to FBI Agent Grahm Coder, Discovery Documents, page 1236

Watts uses the colorful term "walking on eggshells" [around Shan'ann] in his first go-round with the cops in August 2018, and it crops up again in the second go-round, in February 2019. What's he talking about?

The term itself refers to broken eggshells lying on the floor and in this case, Watts trying to walk around *in his home* without cracking eggshells. It invokes both the fragility of the folks surrounding him, but also the fragility of the peace. A wrong move, a reckless remark could create cracks and then a cryfest. It's debatable of course, but one could make the case that the Watts children were not as happy or as healthy as many other children, with happiness being a factor of health, and vice versa. Shan'ann's Facebook videos weren't ideal for young children to feel safe, secure or their private and personal needs attended to either.

Besides the physical fragility of the children, there was also a fragility of the mind. We see this on Christmas Eve when Bella howls at the prospect of meeting Santa, and crawls on the floor screaming as her mother pursues her with camera, recording [and ultimately posting] all of it. During the same video Shan'ann complains to her Live audience that her husband – despite her instructions ["he doesn't listen"] – left his other phone in her car, and Shan'ann then has the chore of retrieving it so they can use this as to snap pictures as well. This is despite the fact that the evening and the moment is a wreck – the children aren't *interested* in performing a happy Christmas *spiel* for the camera, let alone two cameras.

The important take-out of this term is that Watts was used to it. He'd been walking on eggshells for most of his marriage. He'd been doing it for years. Stress at home was second-nature. It's because of this that he probably felt prepped and ready to commit murder. If he could walk on eggshells for years trying to *avoid* trouble [and perhaps succeeding in silly areas, and then succeeding in serious areas – like an affair] perhaps he felt he could walk on eggshells for a while in the aftermath to *courting* trouble, and *causing* the disappearance.

There is also something primal about the idea of crushed baby bird shells that invokes crushed children's skulls and an aborted fetus. The walking on eggshells theme echoes in the stomping and shoving required to get the birdlike frames of his small children through the thief hatch and into the large, egg-like tanks fuming with hot, toxic black yolk. This yolk didn't sustain life, it dissolved it, becoming a fuel for homes or cars or city blocks.

Now consider the idea of Chopped Liver walking on eggshells and how self-esteem plays into that. It does, doesn't it?

But when Watts claims he didn't have access to the bank account, he stretches credibility to breaking point. Page 17 of the *CBI Report* deals with this aspect. At around the 4-hour mark of the audio, detective Baumhover peppers Watts with a few questions. One of these is why the Rzuceks moved in with the Watts family in Saratoga Trail in the first place. Let's go there.

BAUMHOVER: *What was their purpose for moving out there?*

WATTS: *They just wanted to be closer to the kids.*

The Rzuceks lived in Colorado – in the basement – for 16 months, because they wanted to be closer to the kids? When Frank Rzucek is questioned about Shan'ann's stay in North Carolina, he stresses that it was originally meant to be a "couple of weeks" stay. Page 680 and 681 in the Discovery Documents reiterates how the stay was planned to be relatively short, but Shan'ann then decided to stay longer. As Frank Rzucek puts it:

"The 6 week trip to North Carolina was the first time they had visited for that long..."

It's difficult to imagine the trip to North Carolina right then, during the first trimester of her pregnancy, wasn't *directly as a result of their worsening financial situation.* Shan'ann's job required her to bullshit about how wonderful her life was, so to admit things weren't wonderful, that they weren't thriving and that they were actually going to lose their big house and their lifestyle [and even the third pregnancy wasn't a fairy tale either] was to admit defeat. It certainly wasn't promotion. But this is the bind that the MLM locked her into.

In the same way, the Rzuceks' extended visit to Colorado in 2015 and 2016 wasn't *really* about family reunions either, was it? Wasn't it because the Rzuceks were also facing bankruptcy themselves? If they were, <u>why not just be honest about it?</u> And why in 2019 couldn't Watts just be honest about it?

Because it's a self-esteem issue. Not having money is a self-esteem issue. Although Watts seems to be fairly forthright about the finances, his casual attitude is misdirection.

I was always just like…just flying under the radar.

I just wanted to be a regular guy…

Watts acknowledges that the Rzuceks even put their house up for sale during their 16 month stint in Colorado, but weren't able to sell it. Perhaps they rented it out. We know for a fact that there was a fair amount of families moving in and sharing the load so to speak. In fact <u>the Rosenberg's were weeks away from moving to Colorado them-selves</u>, and Saratoga Trail was going to be their HQ until they had their shit sorted and settled. Once again, it was Shan'ann snapping the whip. It was her pals who'd be moving in and Watts would just have to deal with it; it was her way or them losing the house.

Under normal circumstances, the Rosenberg's sharing the expenses [paying rent] would be useful and even necessary. But these weren't normal circumstances. Cassie had Shan'ann's back, we know that and if Watts had access to her iCloud, he would have known too. But with her around, actually living with them, it wasn't going to be walking on eggshells anymore, it was going to be *impossible* to pursue an affair with Kessinger.

BAUMHOVER: *So were they trying to move to Colorado, or just…*

WATTS: *They were thinking about it…but they didn't want to leave…They knew their house wasn't being taken care of…They wanted to go back and… They put their house up for sale, for a little while…*

So the Rzuceks seemed about to lose their house at one stage [Watts implies *voluntarily*], and in Spring Lake, over the years money had been disappearing from that house [to fuel an addiction] putting that household in jeopardy, and then the Saratoga Trail house was going to be lost. The Rosenberg's were moving out of their home and into the Watts home. We know Shan'ann and Nickole Atkinson both changed jobs [and quit their jobs] in the last few months of Shan'ann's life.

Just because the Money Narrative isn't mentioned, it doesn't mean it wasn't foremost in people's minds. When we see Thrivers going berserk about luxury cars and overseas trips on social media, it's very public. What we don't see is them losing their shit about not being able to afford long-term airport parking, or scratching their heads over a credit card alert for $68 on a Saturday night, and resolving to hold onto the receipts.

We get a glimpse of the actual dire straits acknowledged by both Shan'ann and her husband on page 2098 of the Discovery Documents. It's before 05:00 on July 31st, and they're bickering about where he parked the Lexus:

SHAN'ANN: *You never ever listen to me. How much a day?*

WATTS: [Sends a photograph of the parking signs]: *$16*

SHAN'ANN: *Which lot?*

WATTS: *east economy lot.*

SHAN'ANN: *$130 we can't spend at the beach.*

In his interrogation from prison, Watts lays the blame for their financial problems at the door of credit card debt. He says he never thought they would have to file for bankruptcy. But when all your credit cards are maxed out, so much so that you're using gift cards to buy meals and what not, and this is three years after the first bankruptcy, are you really in the dark about just how messed up your financial situation is?

WATTS: ...*It's just like, I don't know how long it was gonna take... But apparently it was...[garbled] never get out of it. That's what it felt like.*

LEE: *Weren't you guys behind on your mortgage payments?*

WATTS [Sighs]: *Yeah. Earlier...December 2017, to January, February, March 2018. That's when I took-we took the 401K out. That was all...to pay for that.*

CODER: *How was it that you spent so much money?*

WATTS: *Just...you know...kids. Just other bills that we had. And I dunno-I mean, I knew the car was being paid for, by Le-Vel, but I never really asked to see, like-I mean I never really had access to the bank account on my phone.*

CODER [Unconvinced*]: *Oh.*

WATTS: *I never really asked to see what it looked like. From my little 4-wheeler incident, where I sold it [for less] without paying it off, and she thought I'm never going to touch the account, ever.*

Although the interrogators chuckle at this, it's plausible that Watts is lying about his obliviousness to the bank account. The home loan was in his name for Pete's sake. He claims he didn't have access to their bank account *on his phone*. Watts is a goofball in many ways, but he's savvy when it comes to tech, to technical information and numbers. Even though he was cash-strapped, he was able to make the affair work for a few weeks [without Shan'ann knowing] by juggling Anadarko gift cards. That shows some ingenuity.

I was always just like…just flying under the radar.

I just wanted to be a regular guy…

We see how well he was able to keep track of his secret stash of nude selfies on his phone, and just how on the ball he was in getting to grips with the finances [calling the realtor and the school] within hours of disposing of the bodies. He also called the bank on the afternoon of August 13th.

So regardless of whether he had access to their bank account on his phone, they would receive account notices from their bank in the mail, there was online banking he could do on his work computer or the laptop at home. And if he really had his hands over his ears, Shan'ann would be barking at him incessantly to remind. So his lack of knowledge in this area is a ruse to hide not only the premeditation aspect, but also Watts' low self-esteem and cowardice in dealing with a steadily worsening situation.

But there's a difference in saying Watts was unaware of the finances because he didn't have access, and saying Watts didn't have access so he was unaware. It does seem credible that he didn't have access, not necessarily that he couldn't see or couldn't access their bank account, but that he didn't have control over it. It's likely also that his lack of control wasn't because he was locked out, but simply that Shan'ann was running the show and if he interfered she would have a fit. There is a world of difference between not having access and having access but being too terrified or too bullied to do anything about it.

A premeditated murder would of course restore that access, in the sense that he could regain financial control over his fate with immediate effect. If Watts was fully aware of the true extent of their financial disaster, and space had been afforded to figure that out by virtue of Shan'ann's stepping out of the house for five weeks, along with the financial imperatives associated with maintaining a mistress for six weeks [all that wining and dining], then we can see how Watts may have felt desperate to hold onto his control of his pay check, his life, his house and his newfound freedom.

What's easy to miss as we align our psychology with Watts is Shan'ann may have felt perfectly justified in keeping Watts' paws off the piggybank given the situation with his father, and his addiction. Shan'ann may have felt herself more qualified and responsible to deal with money, but was she? Or was control over the family finances [which despite her efforts had spiralled completely out of control] just another symptom of OCD. Doesn't the financial failure of the Watts money pot reflect something else: The failure to tame a capricious world filled with wild and untameable animals, while conducting a love affair with unrealistic fairy tales and magical thinking?

*Coder's misgivings about Watts' answer makes sense. In early police reports, cited by _CBS Denver_ on November 21st [following the release of the 2000 pages of discovery], there's a compelling snippet near the end that doesn't make any sense.

Chris Watts told officers when they first searched the house that "…he couldn't log in to check the bank accounts because she does the finances. He said **he knows the password but not the user name.**" The report continues, "Chris advised if there was a stock pile of cash in the house he would not have known about it."

There are many instances where users forget their passwords, and it's usually a simple process to retrieve them. The same applies to usernames. Watts appears to not want folks to know Watts had access not only to the bank accounts but Shan'ann's phone [and iCloud] as well. He had access to everything else, and was able to recite many passwords from memory during the first interrogation, including for the Vivint security system, the router, the laptop Shan'ann used as well as the iPad and iWatches.

The Automatic Payment

"Coincidences mean you're on the right path." —
Simon Van Booy, Love Begins in Winter

I n true crime there are no coincidences. What was your gut feeling when you first learned of the denied credit transaction on the morning of the incident? Mine was that it was *very* significant. In fact I was almost certain Watts himself had done a "test" in order to check whether there was any money on Shan'ann's card. While I no longer feel that's the case, and while *some* fine-tuning is necessary and essential through the course of eight books on this case, the denied credit card remains hugely significant.

Baumhover also thought so, which is why he brings it up at some length during the Second Confession interview. The detective also highlights this area on page 554 of the Discovery Documents. Let's start there, review what he said then, and then look at his remarks a few months later, confronting Watts in person at Dodge prison.

Baumhover advised he had been hand searching through Shan'ann's cell phone looking for information related to the disappearance. [The detective] advised he [observed] an email received by Shan'ann [on her phone] on Monday, August 13th, 2018, between 2:00-2:50 A.M. advising her that her credit card had been denied.

This timestamp appears to be an error – we'll deal with in shortly.

[The detective] advised it appeared Shan'ann was attempting to purchase some haircare products the morning she had returned. Baumhover stated **the Watts family appeared to be living beyond their means and were possibly having serious financial issues.** *Baumhover stated it seemed odd* **Watts wanted to talk more about his financial situation than the fact his wife and daughters were missing.**

What we see here from the lead detective is he walks into the Watts house completely cold, and within moments of finding out about the denied credit card he surmises the family are living beyond their means. It follows directly in terms of the discovery narrative, in the terms Baumhover frames the situation in. Baumhover doesn't simply say the family seemed to be struggling financially, it's described as something a lot more serious. He goes further to not only emphasize by juxtaposing the financial malaise with Watts' inability at the scene to focus on the fact of the actual disappearance. He seems preoccupied with the serious financial situation, as though the serious financial situation is more serious than the situation involving his family.

And ultimately, in terms of his priorities, this is absolutely true. In a horrible way Shan'ann, the third pregnancy, his two sickly children and their ridiculously expensive school fees all boiled down to one thing – expenses. Expenses he felt he could no longer afford. And in the narrow snapshot of the denied credit card – flagging on the very night of the disappearance – the seriousness is exposed and confirmed.

Naturally there was another way for Watts to determine the exact state of their finances. He didn't have to attempt a transaction to see if it bounced. He knew, through his entrepreneurial use of gift cards, just how limited his options were. Further, he knew that on Saturday night the gift card option was no longer an option. If Watts wanted to see how much money there was left, all he had to do was draw money [which he did on Saturday night, to pay the babysitter] and look at the receipt. Or look online. The question is, did he look just after he killed Shan'ann, or shortly before, or was that very much part of the premeditation?

Given that Watts told Kessinger he intended to find an apartment, and even provided her with a budget, it's certain Watts had to check his balance sheet to see what he could afford. He may have changed his mind about moving as more information became clear about just how serious the finances were. It would have been a major blow, for example, to find out Shan'ann's HOA payments had been going to the wrong address for an entire year [*CBI Report*, page 17]. But if he *already knew* they were behind on their mortgage payments, and it appeared he did know, perhaps he knew about the HOA, and it formed a backdrop, a slow dripping of the tap that was becoming harder and harder to handle.

The denied credit card on the night of the incident simultaneously confirms the degree of their financial malaise and raises the question: to what extent did Watts know about it.

The fact that he could commit triple murder and have the presence of mind to begin financial clean-up operations before the blood of his family was even cold – I believe – answers that question.

But let's listen in on Watts and get a feel for the relevance of the automatic transaction.

BAUMHOVER: *There's a haircare company – I think it's called Monat. Does that ring a bell?*[*]

It should. Monat was just another MLM company Shan'ann was using.

WATTS: *Haircare? No.*

The detective is quite clever in how he asks Watts about the transaction. He does it tactically by starting off indirectly. He asks Watts if knows about Monat first. If he says yes it's easier to get him to acknowledge knowledge of the transaction itself. Notice Watts cottons-on to the haircare bit of the question without seeking clarification on the MLM company.

BAUMHOVER: *Like maybe hair...maybe hair dye? I don't know. It looks like a...um...*

WATTS: *Umm...*

BAUMHOVER: *Do you know if she did like an auto order...through that company? Had stuff delivered? For hair? Any kind of haircare products or haircare dye?*

WATTS [Long pause]: *She had some...I mean...she had like, little...I know there was something, like a little gift packs she had delivered like...once, every once every month, every two months. It had like a different array of products in it.*

This is already a departure from Watts' initial denial. He's asked about haircare ringing a bell, Watts says no, and suddenly – when pushed, when it's clear the detective knows something about what he's asking about – Watts remembers.

BAUMHOVER: *Don't remember where it's from?*

WATTS [Another long pause]: *No. Like you said...Monay?*

BAUMHOVER: *Monat. [Spells it out]: M.O.N.A.T.*

WATTS: *Mm-mm. [Softly] Doesn't ring a bell.*

So now Baumhover addresses the real question. He doesn't really care whether Watts knows about the haircare company, he cares about this part. But if he did know about the company, Watts would be cornered somewhat, pressured to acknowledge knowledge.

BAUMHOVER: *There was a...there was an order that was made... like 02:51...that's why I ask. If it was like an auto-order type thing.*

WATTS [Recognizing what Baumhover's getting at]: It *might have been auto-order.*

BAUMHOVER: *Yeah.*

WATTS: *It might have been something that...[Changes direction with his answer]. I know that Nickole Atkinson – she's involved in all that stuff, maybe.*

Watts is not wrong on this score; Atkinson is a part-time hairdresser, and she's often showing off a colorful new hairstyle on social media. Atkinson can be seen in court – at the sentencing hearing – sporting bright purple hair, while Frank Rzucek has a sweater on [removed when he read out his statement] with color-coded the hashtag #ShinelikeShanann.

WATTS: *Maybe Shan'ann got her...maybe she got something [from Atkinson] or maybe it was something she recommended.*

BAUMHOVER: *Okay.*

Whether Watts knew the extent of his wife's love affair with MLM companies isn't touched on here, and for my money, isn't dealt with in nearly enough detail.** The exact extent of the credit card debt also isn't discussed in precise terms. Maybe Watts really didn't know how deep in the quagmire they were [in terms of the credit cards]. If he didn't know, he wouldn't be the first.

The "invisible" nature of the 02:51 transaction also illustrates the stealthy, almost secret way the MLM's subtract money from their members. Think about it. 02:51 on a Monday morning in the middle of the month. Isn't this the best time, *** when one is least likely to be awake, and most distracted the next morning [a Monday morning] to notice or care about money leaking out of an account? Especially if it's by auto-order.

The auto-order confirmation also blows out of the water the myth that Shan'ann was home after her flight, awake and shopping online firsthand. Despite the fact that she'd been on a long flight, and one delayed by several hours, and her husband's affair, some believed it was more likely Shan'ann made the purchase than that Watts did. Well, they were right, Shan'ann did make the purchase but she wasn't awake *or alive* when she made it.

*Monat started operating in 2014. By March 2018 over <u>500 complaints had been filed against the company</u>. According to KNTV three class action lawsuits have been filed against Monat alleging hair loss, scalp irritation and scalp injury.

**Watts' direct experience with Thrive is touched on by investigators, and will be examined later on in this narrative.

***There's an impression that by doing these transactions at these times, the customer isn't "awakened" or "disturbed" to notice them and perhaps put a stop to them. The credit card culture we live in does that. The very idea of money is reduced to a fiction as one card after another can be charged and stuff magically [if temporarily] afforded. This strategy – and it is a strategy – serves to protect the self-esteem attached to having things and having credit, even when one's credit has run out.

The First Time Kessinger Mentions Shan'ann's Pregnancy to the Feds

*"What's money? A man is a success if he gets up in
the morning and goes to bed at night and in between
does what he wants to do." — Bob Dylan*

L et's step out of the *CBI Report* and return to the interview that
really set the cat between the pigeons. If *this* interview didn't
take place when it did, everything may have turned out differ-
ently.

At midday on August 15th, 2018, Nichol Kessinger gave her first interview to law enforcement, <u>close to her father's home</u>. <u>Two FBI agents</u>,
Mark Lehrer and Philip Jones were present, as was her father.

This interview was described recently as <u>the "bombshell" that revealed Watts as a suspect</u> in the disappearance of his family, and also
provided the cops with the certainty that Watts [who was being poly-
graphed *at the same time*] was dissembling. It certainly was a bombshell. When Watts was done with the polygraph, irrespective of the
results of the polygraph, Coder and Lee tag-teamed Watts, hitting
him hard with the fact that he was lying, and doing so by confronting
him with the affair. Kessinger confirmed the scale and scope of Watts'

culpability – it was far more than he was letting on. Within hours of Kessinger's interview with the FBI, Watts was arrested and taken to jail.

The intel Kessinger provided not only betrayed Watts but completed wrong-footed him. If he was ahead in the game, or if the game was somewhat even, Kessinger tipped the scales against him.

But as we go back in time to that interview, we might as well ask: when is the first moment Kessinger mentions Shan'ann's pregnancy to the cops. It had to register on her radar at some point, and when it did, it had to matter. She was in a relationship with a married man. So, what did she think about his wife being pregnant? Did she know? When she did she know? How did she react? How did she feel about it? What did he tell her about it? What did she say in response? How did she deal with it? How did she deal with it to law enforcement?

AGENT [Referring to Kessinger's two telephone conversations with Watts late on Sunday night, August 12th and late on Monday night August 13th]: *Did anything jump out at you during that conversation? Had anything changed? Was anything different now?*

KESSINGER [Indistinct]: *No. We were flirting. I mean, I was worried too. I just didn't...I just thought she left that day. That's really what I thought. And then [inaudible]...oh, maybe this is quite serious...and I knew they were going through a separation...[but] the fact that all the stuff was still there, that was weird.*

Bear in mind the interview with the Feds is on a Wednesday, the Sermon on the Porch was on Tuesday, but Facebook was already buzzing about the disappearance, and the fact that it was a pregnant mother and her two daughters missing, on Monday afternoon and night. When Kessinger is asked whether anything jumped out at her during the conversation, Kessinger claims – not entirely convincingly – that they were still flirting even after she learned Shan'ann and the kids were missing. It's not so much that they weren't flirting, maybe they were, it's this idea of them flirting even though the knowledge that Shan'ann was pregnant was already out there. It suggests [and this is just a guess] that Kessinger may well have known about the pregnancy prior to the disappearance. She may have spied on Shan'ann on Facebook,* and when the profile picture and videos appeared on the public profile about the pregnancy, she may have confronted Watts.

Watts had lied about talking to Shan'ann about a separation and a divorce [the first sprinkling of salt on the seeds of this idea only occurred in North Carolina as late as the first week of August], so it stands to reason – if the pregnancy came up – Watts lied about that too.** He may have told Kessinger the child wasn't his and that's why they were getting divorced. And theoretically, that could explain where she'd gone with the kids – to *him*.

The question is when. When did Watts tell Kessinger about the pregnancy? One possible clue to this lies in the answer to the question of when Kessinger mentioned the pregnancy to the Feds for the first time. Let's go back to August 15th.

AGENT: *And did he tell you anything that was going on with her? Was she seeing anybody or…Had she talked about plans…what she was going to do? That she was going to leave…going to some place else?*

KESSINGER: *As far as I knew…um…we kept it pretty short and sweet. If she ever came up in conversation…he was very…civil about her…like…he never had anything negative or derogatory to say about her. He just told me they were separated, and this is why [voice goes up], and…that was about it. And then…then…*

AGENT: *Did he say why? Did he say what the reason was…?*

KESSINGER: *Why they were separated? [Voice rises]. He just said they weren't [indistinct] very well any more. I don't know...financial... [indistinct mumbling]...so he wasn't just...negative about her. And that was something pretty unique about our...about what he had going on. So you know...and I know she was a good mom...*

It's strange that she doesn't bring up the pregnancy as a significant issue for her. As the mistress of a married man, it should be uppermost in her mind. Unfortunately the audio is seriously garbled so it's impossible to get clarity on her responses. But it doesn't sound like the pregnancy comes up, does it?

AGENT: *Did he ever say he wasn't in love with her anymore?*

KESSINGER: *[Garbled response]...This is a horrible situation, and I don't know where she's at. It's not okay.*

AGENT: *...and we are too, and obviously want to get to the bottom of this. And that's...that's why some of the questions I'm gonna ask are... just trying to get to the bottom of this. And so, when he told you that he was in love with you, was that recent...? Was that...uh...right away? Was that July or...?*

KESSINGER: *It was probably a couple of weeks ago.*

AGENT: *And did you talk about...I'm in love with you now...and I want a life together?*

KESSINGER [Voice rising]: *I think we did talk about the future. I think all couples do talk about the future, but it was never like, [sing-song dramatic voice], 'Hey, I'm like leaving her. We're going to get a house together. You're moving in with me.' It was never like this very forward [or formal?] thing. And you know, I even told. I said...if you're getting a divorce, you've been married for a long time, I think it would be wise for you to spend a lot of time on your [voice rises to a high pitch] own. And I recently got out of a relationship this year, and I also think it's healthy to spend time on my own. And like...I...I respect monogamy...*

The reader is encouraged to listen to the rest of the tape and draw your own conclusions.

What we do know is the pregnancy was discussed the next day, a Thursday, quite late into Kessinger's interview with FBI Agent Kevin Koback. That interview commences on page 568 of the Discover Documents. It takes two-and-a-half pages of summarised audio to reach the point where the pregnancy comes up for the first time.

When Kessinger is asked how she found out Shan'ann was pregnant, Kessinger says she read about it in newspaper articles on Monday and Tuesday. It's unfortunate Koback doesn't press her for specifics, though it's likely that she would have read about it online, like most people would. But this is assuming she really did only learn about the pregnancy *after* the disappearance.

Watts was terrified at the prospect of having the gender reveal broadcast on social media. The gender reveal was imminent, perhaps even scheduled for Monday,*** the day she was returning to her regular life, and the day he murdered Shan'ann.

Had the gender reveal happened he would have been expected to make an appearance, which would have irrevocably confirmed not only the paternity of the child to Kessinger but also that Watts and Shan'ann *weren't* on the brink of a divorce after all. The pregnancy was ultimately what was going to expose Watts as a liar, not only to his wife, but to his mistress as well.

The irony is <u>Shan'ann and her pals had resolved not to post any-thing on Facebook</u>. But if Watts was monitoring the iCloud, then he knew the secret was out already. Sara had been let in on it, and at 06:51 on August 10th, Josh contacted Watts directly to congratulate him.****

*The idea of Kessinger monitoring Shan'ann on Shan'ann's Facebook isn't unfounded. There is at least one Facebook search by Kessinger for Shan'ann Watts. It took place while Watts was away in North Carolina, on August 4th, at 14:10 [Kessinger also searched Watts' Facebook on that occasion].

And according to her own cell phone records, Kessinger Googled Shan'ann Watts as early as September 1st, 2017. This is also the first entry of the Phone Data Review [Discovery Documents, page 2082].

**The notion that Watts lied to Kessinger about another man being the father of his child isn't unfounded either. On page 575 of the Discovery Documents, Kessinger claims in an interview with FBI Agent Kevin Koback [on August 16th, 2018] that <u>she "challenged" Watts about Shan'ann being pregnant</u>. According to Kessinger, Watts told her the baby wasn't his, wanted to know if everything was still okay with their relationship, and this conversation occurred *after* the disappearance. Kessinger claimed her response to this admission was to cut ties immediately. According to the Discovery Documents, Kessinger's reaction was specifically this:

[Kessinger asked Watts] to delete his text messages to keep their relationship secret from his friends. Kessinger told [Watts] to [only] contact her after his family is found. [By] this time [Kessinger] started to think Watts] had hurt his family as he lied to her, and Shan'ann had not returned…Kessinger…was scared because she did not know who [Watts] was anymore.

In March <u>*Dr. Phil* provided a paternity report</u> proving Watts was the father of the unborn child. The fact that this story was still circulating months after the fact also reinforces the notion of a rumor that Watts wasn't a father, a rumor that – if it were true – may have been encouraging for a mistress embroiled in an affair with a married man.

***The gender reveal party was originally meant to be an actual party held over the following weekend after Shan'ann's return from Phoenix. When Watts expressed his reservations with Shan'ann, it was cancelled. The two then agreed, instead of the gender reveal party, they'd go on a weekend trip together – to Aspen – to work on their marriage. It was then decided that there wouldn't be a party, but also that the gender reveal would be moved possibly to Monday [based on one interpretation of the text below].

August 9th, 22:27, text from Shan'ann Watts to Sara Nudd:

I want to tell you gender, but you have to keep secret. He wants to wait till I'm back [from Phoenix] to tell everyone. So Monday. [Discovery Documents, page 2109]

****The text from Cassie Rosenberg's husband Josh congratulating Watts on his baby body is cited on page 708 of the Discovery Documents.

LIES

"I will call him [Ronnie] and tell him what I think about this. It's not fucking cool at all because it is the kids. I will set this right." — Chris Watts in a message to Shan'ann regarding Nut Gate at 20:16 on July 9th, 2018 [Discovery Documents, page 2085]

Tammy's Polygraph

"Truth came out last night. I didn't create no dagger between you and your dad. That was done by your mom and your dad and I won't change a thing."
— *Shan'ann Watts' text to Chris Watts, August 4ᵗʰ, 2018, 03:36 [Discovery Documents, page 2099].*

There are rare moments of authenticity to be found in the five hours of discussion recorded that February day inside that icy prison. Ironically, they're the moments when Watts isn't on stage being examined about something, but when Watts talks candidly about lying.

LEE: *What did you think of the polygraph?*

WATTS [Straight-up]: *It was horrible.*

Coder chuckles.

WATTS: *I dunno-I dunno how you do that?*

LEE: *Why do you say that?*

CODER [Keeping it light]: *Because Tammy's a torturer...*

LEE [Smiling]: *I am not...*

The polygraph report Lee compiled spans 34 pages. The entire Second Confession conducted between three questioners that day, barely reaches 29. Both reports were authored by the same person so there is no discrepancy there. The polygraph *was* torture, and the incredible thing about it was Lee's ability to concentrate and maintain the pressure on Watts. Much of this was using a very simple ingredient: time.

It was effectively one woman against one man for several hours, although realistically that woman was well rested, and armed to the teeth with intel, whereas Watts had little to eat and little to work on but guile, and going with his gut, and neither of those were up to snuff. Watts had likely also not slept well for the previous several nights or even longer, and a case could be made that he had no Thrive patches handy as the final hours wore on to hone his dullard mind. He was like wearing the same shoes for hours on end. The body underneath loses its shine, its sharpness, and goes soft. Ironically, Watts was wearing the same clothes for a few days on end. Usually in situations like that, simply sitting and waiting at an airport for a transfer [as I've recently done] is exhausting, never mind facing intense questioning at the same time that you're going nowhere.

If Watts flattered himself into believing he could bamboozle his wife for weeks, and manipulate his mistress into falling for him, or that he was so crafty he could lead many others down the garden path – such as his co-workers at Anadarko – law enforcement is a different kettle of fish. The FBI *isn't* MLM. It's not a crowd that's going to tell you what you want to hear. It's not a crowd that's gullible to bullshit, or can't tell the difference, in fact, precisely the opposite.

An FBI agent isn't like a family member asking if you took out the trash. The FBI isn't like some mistress or some person compromised by emotion or family ties. Even so, Watts seemed to back himself. Big mistake. But the reason why it was so horrible wasn't so much because of Lee, but simply because she gave him all the rope he needed to hang himself, and he asked for a *lot* of rope.

When we saw Lee, shortly after the polygraph, informing Watts why his performance wasn't convincing, he wanted to know because he didn't know. She told him he hadn't shed a single tear. He reasoned that he wasn't grieving because he was still hopeful that his family was okay. And so this was the crux. He was trying to influence them by talking to them, by trying to bullshit, and the more he tried, the more he was also finding out what *they* knew. Thing is, they weren't on trial for triple murder, he was, and if they found something out there was a lot more at stake for him than if he did.

But a significant part of the polygraph *was* a trick. Here's why…

WATTS: *You asked me questions before the polygraph for like three to four hours beforehand…and then you do the polygraph. You just break down somebody's brain…to…*

LEE [Smiling]: *To mush or what?*

Raucous laughter erupts in the background. Polygraphs don't have to be conducted like that. The polygraph of Adam Shacknai, for example, took only a handful of minutes. The polygraph tests of the Ramseys [not that these are exculpatory by any means] were similarly brief. An FBI polygraph can lead to interrogations that take hours, but this is at the discretion of the examiner, and Lee – although a CBI agent – used it. And it worked.

WATTS: *To mush. Jello. I know it's just like…it's…you guys have a job and a plan, and you executed it.*

One of the mindbender Lee might do to Watts is to give him a question and then instruct him to purposefully lie about the answer. The mindfuckery comes in where the liar is now knowingly lying and the polygrapher knows he's lying, and now he has to try to act the part that the lie should cause some kind of reaction. Inwardly this sews doubt even with a silky smooth dissembler.

WATTS: *Like, I kinda knew like…when she asked about Saturday night, and the Rockies Game, I knew it was going to be a through interview.*

And yet the polygraph questions were few, and none of them had to do with Kessinger.

They were:

Did you physically cause Shan'ann's disappearance?

Now, because Lee had seeded his mind previously with this question, asking him to open up his mind and imagine different ways someone might disappear, and really fleshing it out, it meant she was leading him down a path that would inevitably cause him to cross paths with a visual of what did happen [if he was guilty]. Then, when the question is asked, it triggers a richer experience [assuming it's there, and – well – it was].

Are you lying about the last time you saw Shan'ann?

Do you know where Shan'ann is now?

None of these questions intuit murder, but they do imply the suspicion of *involvement* of some kind, and harm. The second question is the most specific of the three, and is probably based on Lee's intuition that in this area in particular – Watts' dodgy version of his last conversation with Shan'ann – Watts is the most unreliable, and the least honest. That should say something to us today about what we should think not only of the First Confession, but the Second, and also what the cops really think of his stories.

Watts' arrogance during the Sermon on the Porch seemed to infect him, as his conceit only grew worse. But the game wasn't one-sided. It wasn't just Watts losing the plot, it was the reporters, officers and Feds figuring out the game he was playing and playing dumb themselves, and playing along. More than six months down the track, even with the benefit of sober hindsight, Watts doesn't seem to have learned his lesson. His conceit, if anything, has grown, in lockstep with his notoriety.

On page 23 of the *CBI Report* the question is posed:

Did Watts know he would confess to what happened when he walked into the police department that morning?

On paper, it's a ridiculous question. The psychology – the mind-fuckery behind it – is sound, though. It's a question to test humility versus arrogance, lessons learned versus criminal thick-headedness. Watts responds that he knew there was a reason he was brought back to the cop shop the next day.

It doesn't really address the question, does it? The answer ought to be: *no, he didn't expect to confess or be arrested.* He feared that outcome but he thought he might have a chance. We know he thought this because when challenged to take the polygraph, he took it, and when confronted afterwards that he'd failed it [spectacularly, all of it], Watts replied:

I didn't-I didn't lie to you on that polygraph, I promise.

Lee told him they needed to talk now about what actually happened, and as he responded, Coder gently stopped him and told, "Chris, just stop. It's time." Watts was told to take a deep breath, and the reason he was staying was because "he knew he needed to get everything off his chest…" [Discovery Documents, page 599]. And then Watts fell for that as well.

He seemed to be trying to please his interrogators, trying to win them over, not just so he could win his freedom, but bizarrely, in an almost existential sense – as though he really cared about their opinion of him. And this is what sank him.

The last sentence of the section on polygraphs on page 23 of the *CBI Report* quotes Watts verbatim.

WATTS: *Walking in there that day, just walking into that room, I knew I wasn't walking out...*

This too sounds rich. It reminds of the whopper Watts dished out shortly before his arrest on August 15th, after revealing where he'd hidden the bodies of his family at the well site:

WATTS: *There's a reason why I didn't...that I came in because, I mean, there's a reason why I didn't come in with a lawyer either...so I just, like, and this is gonna happen so.*

Watts seemed to be saying then that he made an <u>altruistic choice</u> by sitting down and talking for ten hours or more. So why not just give the information in 5 minutes? Why go to the trouble to murder and then go to the trouble to reluctantly confess? His spiel here is that he hadn't gotten a lawyer because when he came in *he intended to help the cops*. It's just the dumbest circular reasoning you've ever heard, but in the context of a dude with really low self-esteem, you kind of want to give him a pat on the back before leaving the room and hurling outside.

It's also a scenario where Watts, at the end of the day *realizes* he's been caught out, he's finally given up incriminating information and so now he's changing tack; he's minimizing the mendacity and scheming – from his side – that led up to it. As crazy as this is, we shouldn't be surprised by it. This is simply Watts reverting to his preferred default setting, one he has known throughout his life, and marriage:

I was always just like...just flying under the radar.

I just wanted to be a regular guy...

Perhaps it was the politeness of these people saying nice things to him, like they appreciated him coming in, and the fact that several people were hanging on his every word that disarmed him. Compared to his experience with Shan'ann, this civility was a new and unusual experience for him, and in a strange, almost ominous way, it felt good [and horrible] to be asked these questions. It's almost as if, in a certain way, he was asking them of himself for the first time. Even if he'd premeditated the crime, he may not have known exactly why he was doing what he was doing, and so, at the same time that he was lying about it, he was also sort of dealing with it – for the first time – if that makes sense. And thanks to the mindfuckery of his questioners, he was sort of testing how the world would judge the appropriateness of his answers. Did that not work? How about this one, it's fine-tuned a little, maybe that little engine will sound better. Does it? No? How about this…?

Why else did he not call an end to it? He could have. He could have asked for a lawyer or asked to leave at any time. But some part of him *wanted* to face questions. The same part of him that felt terrible about his cowardice regarding his wife wanted to prove – going forward – that he was courageous. And so, at the prison in Wisconsin, the cops arrived thinking that psychology was still in place. And it was.

He wanted to talk about what he'd done, although not necessarily be honest about it. He wanted to leave a good impression [while lying]. He wanted to make friends telling people what they wanted to hear about him. Now, as a prisoner he's doing the same thing, even if that meant telling them he'd murdered his pregnant wife and his own children, but *still* lying.

Long Shadows

"I did belittle him..." — *Shan'ann Watts' text to Addy Molony, August 12ᵗʰ, 2018, 09:04 [Discovery Documents, page 2115].*

The Watts case is difficult to understand without understanding family dynamics, and above all, the dynamics operating in Watts' psyche. What shadows were cast long ago by distant authority figures? And how do these shadows get a hold of a person years later? And do these shadows really have anything to do with what a man might do on a seemingly random day near the end of a long summer in Colorado?

When we speak of shadows we're acknowledging the idea of anxiety. Let's first deal with the idea in general terms, then in a few analogies and finally in the context of this case.

1. Anxiety in General Terms

Ernest Becker poses a fascinating question relating to the idea of anxiety in *The Structure of Evil*. He asks:

"Where does the sense of moral obligation come from?"

And further:

"Why does the individual continue to feel obligation even after the early figures of authority cease [to exist]..."

Becker provides some additional context, by putting the question more simply:

"Why does the child carry over his training so religiously?"

There are positive and negative aspects to this, yin and yang, light and dark. The positive aspects are that our parents do teach us or guide us in basic life skills such as walking, eating, talking and attitudes to personal safety [how to cross a street, how to treat strangers etc.] But there are often negative aspects that our parents pass over to us that are unintended, but nevertheless have a lasting aspect. Of these unintended endowments is anxiety.

Anxiety is part and parcel of the human condition, no matter what. No matter how good or bad our parents, and no matter how evolved we are [as their children], anxiety is going to be part of the package no matter what. That's because human beings are conscious creatures. We have the ability to understand intellectually and existentially that we are mortal – that death waits for us. And the result of this realization is anxiety. Whether we acknowledge death as a reality or not, directly or indirectly anxiety bubbles into our reality. Even the denial of our death at some point in time, whether through amnesia, hedonism, finding character armor, scapegoating, projection, transference, anchoring, or the host of things we may do not to deal with death – all of these behaviours are effectively a personal and private idiosyncratic way of dealing with anxiety.

Anxiety casts long shadows in people's lives. We can see anxiety lurking in the background when people make career choices. Anxiety is there when we choose a life partner. Anxiety hovers whenever we make decisions about money. Our ability to sleep at night, and the quality of that sleep, is a function of anxiety. It's fair to say our quality of life day to day, depends on how well we deal with anxiety.

All of this is fair and good, but where does it actually take us, and what do we do with it? We may understand the concept of anxiety, and visualise long shadows creeping into our lives, but what does it mean?

The Watts case offers us a test case to examine this sort of seemingly unfathomable psychology. True crime in general presents us with scenarios where individuals are faced with anxiety and in that given situation, they experience failure. There is failure to adapt, failure to control anxiety, and failure to find convention affirmation in…well… convention. The criminal act is an unconventional act, and it's principally directed at controlling anxiety.

There's some *Rocket Science* in that revelation, so let's put it up again in italics, and review it slowly:

The criminal act is an unconventional act,

and it's principally directed at controlling anxiety.

It may not seem much of a statement that, but consider how that must read, how that must feel, if you're the victim of this "unconventional act". Imagine how it must feel to be Shan'ann lying in a sandy pit, perhaps able to sit up and dust herself off [as a ghost], and contemplate her injuries.

It may seem ghastly and impersonal then, in this respect, to frame the criminal act in such impersonal terms, when the criminal act feels so very personal. But the fact remains, it's an act directed at anxiety, and whether that anxiety is actually resident in the criminal [as a force that has to be reckoned with and resolved in itself] or an external force, it remains *anxiety* that is being controlled in the equation.

In terms of parents, an authority figure may either be a soothing presence or one that aggravates or inculcates anxiety. Becker refers to this dynamic as the child becoming "the reflex" of the parent.

If we think about Chris Watts and his parents, do we see them as soothers or aggravators?

"He was NEVER close to anyone but his dad..." – Shan'ann Watts to Addy Molony, August 12th, 2018 [Discovery Documents, page 2114].

Ronnie's addiction clearly isn't soothing. If he was the more soothing parent, then when Watts got married, and Ronnie struggled to deal with his son's departure from home and from North Carolina, we have a strange transaction where the son is a soothing presence to the father, and vice versa. When their relationship breaks down there is immediate anxiety. Does that make sense?

2. Analogous Cases

In terms of the Rzuceks, it's difficult to think of Sandi as a soothing figure. It seems unkind to say that, because parents may mean well, may care, may pay attention and may be involved in their children's lives, but they may nevertheless cause *more* anxiety than otherwise. An excellent example of this is Patsy Ramsey, and Patsy's deleterious impact on little JonBenét. Patsy's efforts to make JonBenét into her mother's image [as a pageant queen] may have been good for Patsy, but it was *literally* damaging to the little girl's health.

Another useful example of a maternal presence who means well, but causes damage, is the mother of Oscar Pistorius. In a scenario where Oscar had his lower limbs amputated, he very much depended on a soothing presence. When his father abandoned the family, it fell to his mother to be that soothing presence. In many ways his mother may have given her son the tools he needed to deal with his lost limbs, but one has a sense that a brittleness lay buried in that strength, and the strength in a way was a mask which concealed deep insecurity and deep anxiety. By pretending to be able-bodied when he wasn't, one anxiety was magically dealt with, but this denial immediately ushered in *another* anxiety that was even worse. When Oscar's mother died in a tragic medical mix-up, Oscar lost his primary soothing figure. From there his own celebrity became his anchor.

It's through this dynamic that we begin to understand how the ego develops within the child as a sort of living spirit that is who we are, and is also a separate entity. The ego is really the alter ego which deals with anxiety. Another useful analogy is Clark Kent and Superman. Superman deals with Clark Kent's anxiety.

And so with this perspective in mind, we understand what Becker means when he writes:

*"...the superego, or sense of moral obligation, is the very life style that the child follows in order to avoid anxiety **and minimize censure by the adults**..."*

Just as there is physical death for human beings to be aware of and try to avoid, for social animals there is also social death to guard against. For an animal obsessed with symbols, a social death is symbolically just as serious as actual death. And so the ego and anxiety have the same interplay when it comes to social anxiety.

3. Anxiety in the Watts Case

We can examine two strata – two levels – of anxiety in the Watts case. There's the superficial layer. This is the everyday layer. From Shan'ann's side, it's her application of OCD to take control of her world [including her health]. But those controls are efforts at controlling anxiety. What we see with Shan'ann is her becoming increasingly extroverted as she uses Facebook and becomes caught up in the MLM *schema*. This is an ego response, some of it is driven by anxiety, but in the social media context, whatever is already there is simply amplified, including anxiety. There are simply more triggers for everything, not only anxiety triggers but ego triggers too.

At the same time Shan'ann is controlling her anxiety through OCD, and extraversion in social media, she seems to be someone who lashes out with words. She talks about "FLIPPING" in all caps, and Watts and his father refer to not wanting her to "have a fit" as well as "losing it" etc. Even beyond the context of the crime itself, Shan'ann appeared to be able to control her world by losing her temper, or threatening to lose it. And this allowed her to exert control, for example, on Watts. Sometimes the control were softly spoken words – often orders or directives ["Do the laundry," "Get me a glass of wine," "Open the door," "Where's your phone?" etc.]. Other times the control was more mean-spirited ["Fuck him!", "I will sue for full custody," "Find your balls," etc.]

Watts tended to exert control non-verbally. If anything, Watts became more introverted during his marriage, not less. One of the primary ways Watts dealt with his anxiety was through physical exercise, and through sex. Shan'ann too, masturbated to deal with overwhelming pressure.

The second layer to examine anxiety is via the criminal quotient. These are the paroxysm of emotion that fed more directly into and occurred close to the time of the crime. Shan'ann's response to Nut Gate, compared to Watts', is noteworthy. Shan'ann responds with a torrent of hurtful words, and these words have massive consequences for a range of people. The effects of those words are felt. The controls exerted by those words are real. How does Watts respond? He withdraws further from Shan'ann, and instead invests himself more fully in someone else. His outlet is sexual, which is to say *physical*.

In another sense, Watts' response to anxiety is similar to Shan'ann's. After committing murder [which he does non-verbally, and involves the physical effort of making the bodies disappear], Watts talks a lot to the interrogators. But how does he talk? He lies. He minimizes. He does a lot of talking and a lot of minimizing, all of it intended to reduce or control his anxiety. This the symbolic construct coming to the fore – the ego – at work, and it's up to his ego to do all the work.

There has to be a benefit to lying. If telling the truth guarantees a worse outcome, you lie. But why lie *constantly*, about everything, even about things that don't matter?

Somewhere along the line, in Watts' life, he learned the utility of lying. It became something he relied on more and more.

In my own life I've met a few individuals who are habitual liars. They lie about everything, even small, inconsequential things. When confronted about this, there's a strange, craven paralysis. Even when found out they can't stop lying because they don't seem to know how. It's become a habit. They're habitual liars after all. There seems to have been a point far back in time where there was simply a failure to address anxiety, and in this failure, lying became a handy <u>fob</u>. It became a default mechanism.

Lying of course is maladaptive. Once you start, it's hard to stop, because it's so difficult being honest and making the effort and doing the work when you've been on the easy-streets for so long.

Now imagine you live with someone who gets upset about *everything* – literally EVERY THING. You've tried being straight up and casual but quickly learned that there is just no reasoning with this person. There is only escape. There is only saying the more upsetting thing or the less upsetting thing, so you learn to say the less upsetting thing. Regardless of whether it's true or not, *everything* is minimized. Life is just easier that way.

I was always just like…just flying under the radar.

I just wanted to be a regular guy…

Inside the Monster's Mind

"You can be alone! This pregnancy, you have failed to acknowledge it..." — Shan'ann Watts to Chris Watts, August 5ᵗʰ, 2018 [Discovery Documents, page 632]

We've gotten a handle on anxiety within a closed system, for example the gyrations of anxiety between parents and their progeny, and between a couple dealing with anxiety in a different way, in a marriage. We've also seen how the ego develops as a kind of defense mechanism against anxiety, and not atypically, against other egos, that it to say, other people.

One of the reasons those following the Watts case can't fathom why this crime happened is they're unable to see the contest of egos in this case. Without being able to see criminal psychology through the prism of symbolism [as the criminal sees it, through his unique psychology], we'll never be able to understand why. This makes sense. We don't understand why as long as we superimpose our own psychology over and above those of the individuals involved.

But understanding the mechanism between *anxiety and the ego* isn't sufficient to probe inside the monster's mind. What we want to do is feel out this anxiety thing. Comparing anxiety to the death reflex is a clever intellectual trick. It explains the thing without really explaining it. So how do we get to grips with everyday anxiety? And why should we bother?

Let's begin our journey into the monster's mind by going somewhere practical – the kitchen. More specifically my kitchen. I'm using a neutral example out of my own experience to illustrate how the strings of anxiety begin to work on the psyche, so please bear with me. While working on the *TWO FACE* series last year, from September onwards, the kitchen faucet started dripping. This was easily remedied – by simply turning the faucet more tightly, the dripping could be stopped. But as weeks went by, no matter how tightly I turned the faucet, drops of water steadily found their way through the seal.

DRIP

DRIP

DRIP

There were a few easy ways to mitigate the dripping. One could place a dish at an angle underneath the faucet.

DRIP DRIP DRIP became drip drip drip.

Then, overnight, I'd place a pot under the faucet, and the next morning use that water on the pot plants. As weeks went by, the dripping gradually accelerated.

DRIPDRIPDRIPDRIP…

Soon it was a slow trickle of water. It was starting to get noisy too. I'd be upstairs working or in bed and I'd hear a noise, one I didn't recognize, and it would be some sort of water-related sound coming from the basin.

I was reluctant to deal with the situation for various reasons I won't go into here. I will say a relative was the actual owner of the property, and it was that relative's responsibility to fix whatever was broken inside the property. But I was reluctant to contact this relative for reasons I won't reveal. But there was another reason I was reluctant to sort the situation out directly. I suspected bringing a plumber out simply wouldn't solve the problem. Eventually the dripping became intolerable, *maddening* in fact. Such a simple thing left to accumulate, and aggravate, something postponed endlessly, something that was only getting worse, soon became *inevitable*.

One can compare this dripping of the faucet to the debt situation in the Watts home. It was something that they were aware of but were putting off, or were reluctant to sort out because it would mean confrontation. There's also the scenario of dealing with the issue only to find it didn't solve the problem. We don't know whether Watts tried to talk Shan'ann out of continuing to work with Thrive. We do know that Shan'ann's Thrive efforts, certainly her videos and promotion, dipped in the last few weeks of her life. Of course, her final weekend was invested in another expensive trip to Phoenix, to keep the MLM ball rolling.

We can also interpret the dripping in another way. All those belittling barbs from Shan'ann that Watts didn't answer. There are two elements to the dripping equation. The dripping itself [the barbs] and the response to it. One either deals with the anxiety or allows it to continue, and increase.

A third dimension to the dripping is Watts' investment in Kessinger, and hers in him. Each time they kissed or had sex. Each secreted message. Each nude selfie. Each of these elements was a little drop, but cumulatively, it created an untenable situation that had to be fixed.

When I eventually mustered the wherewithal to get a plumber out, it was November, and the problem was pretty bad. As I expected, the plumber struggled. The faucet was 30 years old and the plumber eventually admitted he was unable to repair it. He even used a blow torch to try to loosen a badly rusted washer. Nothing worked. He hammered the stubborn metal with a heavy hammer, making deafening CLANGING noises throughout. Finally he asked me for my permission to break the washer off. It was either that or buying a new faucet. I wasn't opposed to the latter, but it was explained that this wouldn't be a simple process given the age of pipes. I asked the plumber for his advice, and he thought breaking off the washer was the best option, but by doing so, he might break the whole apparatus.

In the end, the plumber succeeded. He managed to break off the damaged part without breaking the section it was attached to.

This, of course, is another analogy for the Watts case, specifically how Watts dealt with his marriage. The right way to have dealt with this issue would have been to contact the owner, replace the whole faucet, and basically have everyone take responsibility. This would be an expensive and somewhat confrontational scenario. On paper quite simple and easy but for various reasons, quite complicated in practice [because of underlying social dynamics].

Replacing the faucet is analogous to getting a divorce. It's the removal of the marriage apparatus so that another apparatus can be installed to replace it. To do that properly requires permission, agreement and a certain amount of expense. While this is postponed, the faucet drips and anxiety gets worse and worse and worse. And the way one tries to cope with it becomes more and more unconventional. And what did we say?

The criminal act is an unconventional act,
and it's principally directed at controlling anxiety.

In the end what was "fixed" here was the "thing" causing the anxiety. In my case, it was getting rid of a rusty washer, but risking causing damage which could have prompted additional measures, including having to replace the whole apparatus.

The fixing of the washer was "the lesser evil", or the less difficult thing, even though in the context of a 30-year-old faucet, the logical and sensible thing to do was simply pay the piper and replace the whole thing. Perhaps because of greed, or pettiness, I used the impasse with the relative to delay, duck and dodge taking responsibility. When I did take responsibility, it involved an unconventional and somewhat rash act. This did the trick though. The dripping has been taken care of, for now.

In Watts' case Shan'ann, the pregnancy and the kids were the rusty washer causing money to flow out of the household. It was beyond his control. The proper way to deal with it, to deal with anxiety, was to get a divorce. But the underlying dynamics, and Watts' personality meant that wasn't an option for him. How he tried to deal with the problem was by dealing directly with the source of his anxiety. By killing his entire family he was regaining control over not only himself, and his pay check, but a long, fraught period of accumulated anxiety.

He didn't want to deal with the situation but as long as he didn't it became more and more maddening, and eventually, *inevitable.* The difference between a "harmlessly" dripping faucet in a kitchen, and the dripping that led to triple murder lies simply in the scale and scope of the anxiety felt by the individual. If you're still not able to fathom why, it's because you're not feeling the anxiety. If you're not feeling the anxiety, it's because you're not allowing the dripping that got to him to get to you.

The lesson in all this – why should we bother with everyday anxiety – is that at some point, anxiety can take control of us, if we're not careful. Controlling anxiety isn't as easy or simple as it sounds. And remember, irrespective of what we do or when, anxiety is a constant. Once one thing is sorted out there will be something else. And there will always be death to deal with, or not deal with. In a real sense anxiety can't be controlled, rather it has to be accepted or soothed. But come hell or high water, anxiety demands to be dealt with, and the sooner the better. When we do, it's *how* we take control of ourselves, and how soon or how late we do, that matters.

The Tale of Two Foxgloves

"No one can tell what goes on in between the person you were and the person you become. No one can chart that blue and lonely section of hell. There are no maps of the change. You just come out the other side. Or you don't." — Stephen King, The Stand

In fairness to folks in a dripping-situation such as the one described in the previous chapter, we live in a *limiting* world. That means it's not just weakness or cowardice that causes us to allow the faucet to trip, or that allows events to worsen and eventually spiral out of control. Yes, sure. Responsibility lies with us, but it doesn't end there. We live in a limiting world in the sense that it's not only self-limiting, but also *limited*, and many limits imposed on us are imposed externally.

Sigmund Freud once referred to "dark, unfeeling and unloving powers" that determine human destiny. So, in the neutral scenario of a faucet left to drip for months, the solution seems simple, and in <u>atomistic</u> terms it is. Just fix the damn faucet! It's when we connect our psyches and psychologies to the broader context, all those messy emotional connections to relatives and owners and contracts and transactions and obligations, then what should be simple becomes fraught, and anxious.

Sometimes the way through this sense of being overwhelmed by the past, and grudges, is to simply turn over a new leaf and be a new person reborn into a new day, and act as if none of those limits apply. That can work but we are naïve if we think pretending they don't exist renders them non-existent.

Let me share a brief anecdote. While researching The Murder of Vincent van Gogh, I was interested in the foxgloves he depicted in Van Gogh's most famous and expensive painting, _The Portrait of Dr. Gachet_. In the foreground Van Gogh painted flowers on an orange table. These flowers are symbolic, used by the doctor medicinally to treat his patient. However, since foxglove [_digitalis_] is poisonous, the results of this poisoning and limiting treatment were [as you can imagine] counterproductive.

In any event, as part of my research I planted foxgloves in my garden – several seeds at once, all over the garden. Then something strange happened. A huge plant began to emerge and beside it another. One of the two was significantly larger than the other, throwing out gigantic, furry, elephant-like leaves. It was looking to become a real monster. Huge. But both refused to flower. A few others, much smaller specimens, pushed out of the soil in other quadrants of the garden. Some of these flowered at their own pace, but the giant stubbornly did not. Would not. It grew bigger and bigger, and then seemed to stand still through winter – waiting, in a kind of self-imposed vegetative stasis.

Finally, when the time was right [based on some unfathomable vegetative consciousness and clockwork] the smaller foxglove expanded again and then sent out a tall, flowery stalk. Big, beautiful pink flowers formed and expanded the way foxgloves typically do. But the even larger behemoth beside it refused to do the same. The plants were _right beside one another_ and one that had seemed to simply be surviving was now thriving, while the other, in slightly less sun but approximately identical conditions, simply remained in its self-imposed stasis. Eventually the second plant did flower, even more spectacularly than its sibling and according to its own agenda, if that's the word.

So where does the magic lie, in the ground or in the seed? Where do the limits lie? Do you see how in this scenario anxiety is justified and so is ego? The plant needs to be anxious about its situation, but its ego must nevertheless be ready to make its push when the time comes, and when it's going to count most.

What this seemed to show is just how peculiar the boundary is between one organism and another, even when it is the same kind of organism occupying the same turf in the same garden. Just the *slightest variation* in light and soil can make a world of difference for the experience of being alive, and how much and when the organism must invest in expanding himself. The environment can be limiting, especially in winter. But other organisms surrounding that organism, and even the soil, can also affect the survival and potential of an organism. Clearly an organism must balance and pace how and when it limits itself, with the opportunities and limits that lie its environment, along with seasonal configurations, and day-to-day weather.

After a few days of bright, flowery abundance the huge monster's journey came to an end. It withered and died, each pink flowery bud transforming into a seed, and each light brown seed apparently filled with the ingredients to perpetuate the monster, and itself, and its poisonous species. I collected these seeds and only these seeds in the hope that the next season's foxgloves would be just as oversized and abundant. But will they?

Now let's apply some of this truth to the texture of the Watts case.

During Nichol Kessinger's earliest interviews with the FBI, with her father present, she admitted she knew why Watts had lied to her.

KESSINGER: *I know why he lied to me. He lied to me because if I'd have known...that...he...had a child on the way...I'd have never wasted my time with him in the first place. Like none of this [speaking in a low tone] would have even have occurred. If he'd have just told me the truth.*

Kessinger doesn't say 'If I'd have known his wife was pregnant.' She doesn't use the word pregnant, she minimizes it to "had a child on the way". She also steers clear of assigning paternity to the child. It's implied, but it's not specified. There's no ownership in terms of it being "his wife" that was pregnant, or "he had a child" or "they were going to have a baby". I do think Kessinger is forthright about the fact of Watts' truthfulness, or lack of. If he hadn't lied to her – about the baby – none of it would have happened. The affair wouldn't have happened, but by the same token, the murders wouldn't have happened either. Conversely, because he was lying about the baby, and because the news of the baby was imminent, and because he knew if she knew she would have dropped him like a hot potato [as she did], he was doing his damnedest to make sure she didn't know. He thought he could do that by controlling the narrative.

KOBACK: *So do you think if he found out that you [catches himself]...um...if...[Interrupts himself, redirects]. Let's say this week, you guys were to go look at some apartments, and this is hypothetical. But you...uhm...**you've never found out** that...his wife was pregnant. Would...would that have changed-changed anything? Um...like you just said. [Roleplaying]: 'If I knew his wife was pregnant, I wouldn't be in this picture.' So if his wife was not pregnant, and um...forgive me, but if-if he takes her out of the picture, you're never going to know...that she's pregnant, right?*

Kessinger asks the agent – softly – what he means. But let's hover for a moment on this idea of her *never* finding out. How realistic is that? Even Watts had to know that it would soon become public knowledge that his wife and family were missing. He *had* to know that her Facebook was public, along with the fact of her pregnancy. So how the heck would Kessinger never find out his wife was pregnant? In addition to this, several of Watts' colleagues knew his wife was pregnant, and some – like Anthony Brown – even knew he was unhappy about the baby and wanted to give it away within the context of apparently flirting with Kessinger at the office.

The idea that Watts's situation at home in terms of the pregnancy, and at work in terms of Kessinger, wasn't a topic of discussion in the office at Anadarko, or out in the field among the rovers, is hard to believe. It's hard to believe Kessinger herself wasn't thinking or talking about it. Within this framework, it's easy to assume that Watts may not have been absolutely clear about the paternity of the baby.

I was always just like…just flying under the radar.

I just wanted to be a regular guy…

In Shan'ann's video posted in early June, Watts doesn't *look* particularly pleased about the pregnancy, and even Shan'ann [out-of-picture] sounds unusually coy and cagey. If Kessinger saw that video, she may have been both conflicted by the announcement, but reassured by Watts sending mixed-messages in the video. And if he told her the baby wasn't his and Shan'ann was somehow manipulating him with the pregnancy, or that the pregnancy was from *her* having an affair, would Kessinger have believed it?

Like none of this [speaking in a low tone] would have even have occurred. If he'd have just told me the truth.

In her exclusive to the *Denver Post*, the key takeout was that <u>Watts had lied to her about everything.</u> The tabloids picked these words as their best headline. And so did TCRS.

He lied about everything...

What's everything?

Did he lie about the fact that he was married? She *knew* he was married and so did all of his co-workers. She knew he was married because his screensaver on his pc at work was of his family. Their first conversations, by her own account, was of his family and his children. But if Watts didn't lie about being married, what did he lie about?

Did he lie about having kids? She knew he had kids. She'd seen photos of them and even at times encouraged him to not spend time with her, but to spend it with them instead.

Did he lie about their finances? Kessinger seemed to appreciate – more than most – the dire financial straits Watts was in. So clearly Watts *didn't* lie about everything, but he did lie about some important issues. What were they?

I was always just like...just flying under the radar.

I just wanted to be a regular guy...

We know he lied about getting divorced. And we know there was a good reason to let that faucet drip. Shan'ann was pregnant and that wasn't going to change. The best he could do was put it off while giving his affair a little time to get off the ground. But the deeper he got into the affair, the more serious the issue of the pregnancy became. And so his anxiety went up a notch, then another, and his ego expanded in step with it.

There *was* a little effort right at the very end to communicate to Shan'ann that he didn't want a third child, and the idea of another baby "scared him to death". On August 8th at 22:19, Shan'ann let Cassie Rosenberg and Nickole Atkinson know that Watts had mentioned getting divorce, but wasn't in a hurry to finalise it.

I will fight for full custody. He told me doesn't want to divorce right away... [Discovery Documents, page 2106].

If Watts had been spying on Shan'ann through her iCloud, this would have told him everything. If he declared war and told her he wanted a divorce, once that step was taken she would take steps.

I will fight for full custody.

I will fight

Fight

Fight

Watts didn't want that, and couldn't afford that. He couldn't afford it moneywise, and if he started the process, probably he wouldn't be able to control a damaging narrative, which would probably send Nikki packing and negate the point of the divorce, certainly this early into his new romance. He wanted to give his relationship time to grow, but to do that, he had to lie about the divorce being finalised [and the pregnancy being either irrelevant or kept secret].

I was always just like...just flying under the radar.

I just wanted to be a regular guy...

But he only got as far as telling Shan'ann a tiny fraction of the truth. He simply said he felt they were incompatible and left it to her to fill in the blanks. In Watts' version he repeatedly claims that even though he didn't admit the affair [just before he killed her], she knew. She just wanted him to acknowledge it. And him not acknowledging it was sort of a way of saying he was afraid to leave the marriage. And thus, a source of hope for her.

They slept in separate beds in the last two weeks of their marriage, so there is a smidgeon of truth to the separation narrative. By all accounts Watts had also mentioned this – the separation – to his parents. But it seems pretty clear he hadn't properly or urgently broached the subject with Shan'ann. Even so, <u>Shan'ann seemed well aware that divorce was looming for her</u>, which is why she had a conversation a few months prior to the murders, and only one month prior to the pregnancy, with Olyinka Hamza.

Now let's listen to Koback's hypothesis again, bearing the above in mind.

KOBACK: *So do you think if he found out that you [catches himself]...um...if...[Interrupts himself, redirects]. Let's say this week, you guys were to go look at some apartments, and this is hypothetical. But you...uhm...**you've never found out** that...his wife was pregnant. Would...would that have changed-changed anything?...forgive me, but if-if he takes her out of the picture, you're never going to know...that she's pregnant, right?*

The answer to this seems to be more a matter that she's never going to know that the baby was his after all. She's going to assume Shan'ann left with the kids to start a new life...with someone else. The real father. And because of the Thrive situation, Shan'ann had to pretend everything was okay at home, and so did he. In other words, this was a mirror for what *they* [he and Kessinger] were about to do, but because he's a victim in this scenario [Shan'ann leaves him, she dumps him*, she cheats on him], so they're justified in doing the same reflexively.

When Kessinger complains that Watts lied about everything, everything seems to refer to just two areas, but unfortunately for her and for Shan'ann, Bella and Ceecee, the things he lied about were the most important things: the divorce and his impending fatherhood. It's clear that the murder took place to prevent either of these realities from intruding. It was important to suppress the fact that he wasn't getting divorced [the process hadn't even started when he said it was almost finished], and the fact that he was about to be a father [which would further invalidate his claim to getting divorced, or that they were even unhappy as a couple, as he claimed].

KESSINGER [Softly]: *What do you mean if he takes her out of the picture? Like...*

KOBACK: *If he murdered her, she's out of the picture. You're never going to know if she was pregnant. If he can get away with murder [stutters], you're not...'I got divorced from my wife...'*

At this point Kessinger's father interjects, and then interrupts again. Now it's Kessinger's father who is trying to stop Koback from "leading", and from Kessinger's point of view, it's important that this narrative is suppressed. Because what if she did know about the pregnancy and pursued the affair anyway? Would anyone forgive for that?

In the Long Shadows chapter we didn't deal with the long shadows of anxiety and how these may have affected Kessinger. She was Bella's age when her own parents divorced**, and like the Watts children, Kessinger was also a sibling to a sister with a similar age gap.

This scenario had the twin impact of making her yearn for a fairy tale life, not only from the perspective of a single adult but from a hurting inner-child point of view. The other aspect is that Kessinger might have felt triggered by fomenting a divorce herself [which she was, in the worst way], and thus potentially repeating and perhaps even trig-gering the same pain and anguish she felt [as a victim] on someone else's children.

[Kessinger] felt bad about not waiting for him to be completely di-vorced...He was in a situation that he was not completely out of yet and she was just coming into it so she did not think it was appropriate to meet his children. [Discovery Documents, page 569].

[Watts] told [Kessinger] he had told Shan'ann he wanted to fix the relationship while in North Carolina [but] Shan'ann said she did not want to try and wanted a divorce. [Discovery Documents, page 648].

**This is dealt with at some length in *TWO FACE, THE MYSTERIOUS MIS-TRESS AND THE CONFESSION.*

Someone Else's Fairy Tale?

"I asked people for water and no one gave me any. People are really obsessed with the summit. They are ready to kill themselves for the summit." — Rizza Alee, a climber from Kashmir

Ernest Becker calls it like it is. In *The Structure of Evil* he describes man as "alone among the animals" as he gradually constructs his "perceptual response world". Becker refers to "imaginative guiding concepts" and an organism that is "continually creating his own reality".

Those are fancy terms for the most human of traits, the same thing that redeems us condemns us – our belief in fairy tales. Fairy tales are *par excellence*, our response to an unknown and often capricious world. We wouldn't need fairy tales if we weren't anxious, and further, if we didn't default to fashioning ego armor around ourselves as an attempt to respond to and control a threatening environment.

The main reason the Watts case has captured our imaginations the way it has – mine, yours, America's, true crime followers around the world – is because it simultaneously corroborates and invalidates the existence and the annihilation of fairy tales. As early as August 27th I was writing about why this particular case fascinated us, and a week before that <u>I provided a WHY, a motive for the triple murders</u>. In a word?

GREED.

This motive was based on ultra-thin-slicing of the case, with very little evidence, information and no interviews besides the Sermon on the Porch. It was based to a large extent on optics, and gut feel.

This is greed in the generalised sense of being materialistic and money-oriented [in face of losing one's home, and not having money greed is a different animal] but also greed in a broader, more symbolic sense. Remember, Watts was greedy in that he wanted to start a new life without any consequences. He wanted to keep his home, as it was, and hold on to his mistress, as she was, and be allowed to continue his life, as he was, without all of this being impinged or eroded or threatened by a bitter divorce dispute.

With Shan'ann, things could get really ugly and really nasty. If she could blow up his parents over nuts, imagine what she could cost him if she went on the warpath once she knew the full extent of his betrayal. And while she was fucking pregnant too!

Fuck him!

I will fight for full custody.

I will fight

Fight

Fight

It's fair to say that merely believing in fairy tales, like many of the Thrivers we see in this story, is very self-indulgent. It's greedy. It's about ego *uber alles*, and when greed is warped and distorted sufficiently, people – egos – will stop at nothing to get their paws on the pot of gold at the end of the rainbow.

Much of the focus of the Watts case, and even the *TWO FACE* series has been on the individuals in this case, and it's necessary to plumb the depths of the identities and psychologies involved. In *OBLIVION* we want to love beyond these people we know. We want to look into society to see how the substrates of culture and community produce selfish, self-indulgent and often deceitful people, but who – to outsiders, prospect Thrive clients in particular – appear as the *perfect* family.

The Watts case reveals the meanness beneath the benign exterior not only of Chris Watts, but the cruelty and nastiness of the culture we live in today. It's a mistake to see Watts as a random aberration. We miss the point if we look at Kessinger and find *her* less than forthcoming. We're close but not close enough to smoke the cigar when we find something wrong with a stay-at-home mom who's on social media constantly, and yet she's regarded as a good wife and mom. What about the company they work for? What about the district attorney and the game they've been playing? There's nothing random about it; the people in this story are an inevitable result of the world as we know it. In a real sense they're puppets on strings, and they simply become the inevitable result of becoming strung out on those strings, the ties that bind.

What I'm angling towards is the reality of a world that is far more limiting than we realize. Its contrivances are far more enslaving than we appreciate. The primary function of culture, as Becker has it, "is to provide for the continuing possibility of self-esteem". In May this year I travelled for several days through the Netherlands, one of the world's happiest, healthiest and [per capita] wealthiest countries. The country is filled with affirming history and art and quaint adaptations to a challenging environment – windmills, bicycles, the world's biggest tulip market. The Dutch also have a distinct personality. They're blunt, they're brash, they're good-humored and generous, they're practical and a little eccentric.

All over Holland I saw obvious traces of goodwill. I saw friends meeting at an open-air pub or on a public train stand and passionately embrace; straight men even kissing one another on the cheek while thumping the other warmly on the back and shoulders. On Friday nights I saw couples returning from a nightclub, well-dressed, cycling home side-by-side on bicycle paths, hand-in hand [one hand on their handlebars].

It's easy to see why the Dutch feel happy in their own skin. They live in a world *they* created, and their culture simply *reflects who they are*. It's not a culture that controls or limits, but one that celebrates, sets free, affirms and as such, places like Amsterdam and the many impressive museums throughout the Netherlands attract tourists – art lovers, hedonists, historians, and curious young couples – from around the world.

If the Netherlands is how culture should be, what's the other extreme? Well, how about Mount Everest? Greed is also the operative emotion on the world's highest mountain. So are the dynamics of ego and anxiety. When these three issues integrate into a dynamic in the highly symbolic arena of "conquering the world's tallest obstacle", we see horrible nastiness flowing out of the bravest and most inspiring fairy tales.

In the midst of men and women strutting their stuff, and proving their heroism, they also reveal how shallow and self-serving we – as modern human beings – have become. We become uncomfortably aware on this highest place on Earth just how low human motivations can go. Lack of empathy – symptoms of a sociopathic society – isn't limited to Chris Watts. Almost everyone on social media seems to be becoming increasingly sociopathic, and Everest is now part of the self-ie-themed shit show that is social media today.

Modern man is a creature, apparently, who couldn't care less, not only about others and the environment, but often *even about himself.* We see that on Everest where climbers start by caring less about their fellow climbers, and end up unable to care about themselves.

We see something similar in Watts throwing in the towel is his own personal Everest seems to float beyond him. He throws in the towel on his own story, and gives in – at 34-years-old – to a life sentence.

Everest provides scale and scope to the elements of culture and society competing for the pot of gold at the top of the mountain. What we see is ego, anxiety and the narcissism trumping it all. Individual desire *uber alles.* We see climbers literally stepping over dead bodies and the dying on the way to their summit selfie, and stepping over the same dead bodies and dying climbers on the way down. Nothing should get in the way of these feelings of self-esteem, and some might say, yes, that's right, that's how it should be.

In the Watts case another fairy tale also didn't want to be interrupted. Anadarko was being wooed by much bigger oil majors, and it didn't want bad publicity surrounding one or two of its staff to ruin the romance.

Watts himself didn't want the pregnancy narrative to ruin his fairy tale. Shan'ann didn't want her Thrive-themed fairy tale ruined by a husband who had no balls, or the fact that she was about to lose her perfect home and perfect family. Shan'ann in a real sense encapsulates the idea of a cultural contrivance that cages and traps those in it. To wit, by dressing Watts up in t-shirts proclaiming himself a proud dad, she was effectively tying him in string and knots, making it hard for him to extricate himself. She was doing the same to herself, too.

If Watts didn't acknowledge his third child, it's also a fact that he didn't feel acknowledged by Shan'ann. What does that mean? He wasn't actually part of her fairy tale. Shan'ann's fairy tale seemed to be about herself, and being a mother and having children. He was expendable in that.

Fuck him!

I will fight for full custody.

In time Watts began to feel the same way. When she cast out his parents, when they became expendable, so did she. How? As soon as he found a new fairy tale in Kessinger, one that *felt* real, she was expendable. The kids were too. And that's what fairy tales do. In our greed for a fairy tale where we get our happily ever after, everything and everyone else is apparently expendable. This is true of individuals in the modern world and corporates. And in this *schema* annihilation is inevitable, *OBLIVION* inescapable.

INSIGHTS AND TERRIBLE NEW TRUTHS

"Bees have to move very fast to stay still." — David Foster Wallace, Brief Interviews with Hideous Men

A Summer of Love

"A stumble may prevent a fall." — Thomas Fuller

At 11:48:58 on August 15th, 2018, Colorado Bureau of Investigation Tammy Lee is sitting opposite Chris Watts in a small interrogation cubicle at Frederick Police Station. On the corner of a grey table polygraph equipment is set up. A laptop is on the table, the screen tilted down but not in the closed position. On her lap, the agent has a clipboard with a short list of questions. The agent is turned in her chair to face Watts, whereas he is facing a wall. Exactly nine hours and thirteen minutes later, at 23:02,* Watts will be asked to stand up and face that same wall he's staring at now, placed in cuffs, and arrested.

It seems a world away, a long time away, but it's only a single afternoon and evening. If Watts can weave the right fairy tale, if he can beat the polygraph and convince the cops he's a genuine guy, then he wins his own fairy tale back. It's important to be explicit about this. In order to win his fairy tale, he has to sell a fairy tale. He has to choose his words carefully. He doesn't just have to make an effort to sell a *spiel*, the cops have to buy it. But can he? Can he pull it off?

Becker would say Watts' problem lies in the fact that he has no authority for his own meanings. What this means is that even in the symbolic sense, when he is trying to construct [that is, fabricate] a fairy tale version of events to get away with murder, he lacks courage and conviction. In other words, even in an invented story, Watts admits his inferiority, his low self-esteem. It's for this reason that he talks with a kind of dumb bravado. He tries to carry it off by sounding casual and suave. This might work on the oil field and to a captive audience of yes-men and women drunk on MLM Kool-Aid. In the context of true crime where there is far more critical thinking, it falls flat, and does so spectacularly.

It's one thing to understand this intellectually, however. To really experience what this looks and feels like, let's go to the beginning of Watts' narrative for his summer with Shan'ann and their folks in North Carolina. Remember at this point he wants to paint a picture of harmony. He wants to sell a fairy tale of a happy family, not only his own family but the extended family too.

Let's listen in.

WATTS: *So we got back from the – we went to that Thrive thing in San Diego. When was that? End of June? And then, I think it was June 26th, that's when we came back here – her dad was watching the kids – and then like, later that same day, they flew to North Carolina.*

LEE [Waving her left hand expansively]: *Okay, so why don't you start...there...and just take me up until [nods] yesterday.*

WATTS: *Okay.*

LEE [Slyly]: *And...with as much detail as you can.*

WATTS: *Okay, so when they were in North Carolina, they were there to see...my family [his voice breaks]...and obviously her family and just kinda like – because they haven't seen the kids in a while. As far as our kids. And so...she had a couple of things she wanted to do there, as far as [holds up his hand to the ceiling] meeting up with her promoters, and customers. She had a bunch of them, in North Carolina. So she told me she could meet everybody else over there, and have like, her dad [lifts his fist to his mouth, seems to choke, reaches for a bottle of water], and mom...and my mom and dad [unscrew the cap of a bottle of water] like...have fun...sort of...with the kids [takes a swig of water].*

Now the reaching for the water is both functional and meant to distract attention away from his micro expressions. Given what he's just done, talking about the mother and father of the woman he's just murdered isn't easy. It's difficult not to give away emotion. It's difficult for something not to leak or slip out. But drinking the water is also functional. It allows him an opportunity to pause, think about what he's going to say, and provide some relief to his dry mouth and throat. In his chest, his heart is beating a mile a minute, and he needs to take a breath to catch his breath.

LEE: *Hmmhmmm.*

Lee mimics Watts by also taking a drink. Her clipboard almost slips to the floor as she leans back. She's also got to be careful to play it cool, keep him engaged and keep him talking. If he says something incriminating she must pretend it's no big deal. She must allow him to craft his fairy tale, and pretend that it's believable, so she can get all the information, including finding the holes and inconsistencies in the fabric.

LEE [Chuckles, referring to the idea of the parents standing in as babysitters]: *Like babysitters, yeah, I get it.*

WATTS [Stutters, pinches his nose]: *...just a vacation, to see everyone, just to see the girls. And Celeste's birthday was during that – on July 17th. So they had a birthday party there...with um [inaudible]...and they FaceTimed me during that...so I got to FaceTime and watch it all, and it was pretty much hanging out with family the entire time.*

Watts doesn't let on that neither of his parents were at the birthday party, and he leaves out Nut Gate, which happened a week and one day prior to the birthday party, on July 9th.

LEE [Nodding]: *Okay.*

WATTS: *And I was just here, going to work and…working out and going running and…just keeping, keeping the house up, and…doing that. Just [stutters]…my flight was July 31st…*

Slow down cowboy. Notice how Clear Watts is on scheduling details. He's fairly vague on all the other details, but he's specific on the dates. The date they returned from San Diego, the date Shan'ann flew to North Carolina [pertinently "the same day"], the date of Ceccee's birthday, the exact date when he flew to North Carolina. Watts distils the entire summer romance with Kessinger into two lines of vanilla text. It's interesting the words he uses to describe the house.

…keeping, keeping the house up…

It seems to be a kind of psychological code for doing what he needed to do to make sure he didn't lose the house. Besides the debt side of the equation, *keeping the house up* also speaks to the idea of keeping things going, keeping up appearances, maintaining a façade. He was certainly trying his best to keep things going with Kessinger in spite of the pregnancy coming along to 10, then 11, then 12, 13, 14, 15 weeks.

…keeping, keeping the house up…

And part of this included his commitment – at least in theory – to Kessinger to move out of the house, and for them to find an apartment for him to stay in, since the marriage was going to end imminently.

…keeping, keeping the house up…

WATTS [Referring to his summer with his family in North Carolina]: *...my flight was July 31ˢᵗ...and I flew out there for a week. Then I-I...I flew out there so I could fly back with them.*

Although Watts is just spinning a tale where nothing much happens [a tale purposefully contrived to be devoid of red flags], he gives away his feelings here. When he describes going to North Carolina, he immediately juxtaposes that with coming back. This is precisely how Watts felt. The moment he left Kessinger he was counting down the days, hours, minutes and seconds when he would be back, and they could be together again. And we know when Watts was in North Carolina, he wasn't really with Shan'ann or the kids. He was on his phone, enjoying secret nude selfies and carefully hiding each one away.

On August 2ⁿᵈ, possibly while at the playground in Myrtle Beach [where Watts is seen preoccupied on his phone] Watts was sending images to Kessinger. On the same day Watts transferred eight images to his Secret Calculator app [Discovery Documents, page 2099].

We know at 23:00 on August 9ᵗʰ, Watts transferred six images, several nude or semi-nude of Kessinger, into his Secret Calculator app. We also know he transferred an enormous tranche on July 31ˢᵗ during his flight to North Carolina. Even on August 14ᵗʰ, Watts was still transferring nude photos of Kessinger into his Secret Calculator. [Discovery Documents, 2097, 2110 and 2128].

WATTS: *So we went...so July 31ˢᵗ...I got there...stayed at her mom and dad's house. The next day we drove to the beach, stayed there...for about four or five days.*

He's leaving out the fact that he didn't sleep in the same room, or bed, as Shan'ann, on that first night, and that Shan'ann began to feel ill when he arrived.

WATTS: *And we...first time the kids had seen the beach. So they were ecstatic, obviously, seeing waves. Being-being in the sand. They love sand. Unfortunately they love sand, because [throws his hands into the air] when you get back, you've got to shower them back.* Ceecee was so into the sea that her bathing suit was just full of seashells.

Lee chuckles.

WATTS [Laughs]: *I was just like, okay, let's get all this off you and rinse you off. But yeah. [Sighs]. It was an awesome trip, like...like just seeing them react to the ocean and [gestures] then...there was like an outdoor mall, and they got going on these little [gestures with arms raised to the ceiling]... like where they strap you to a harness...and kids just get to jump and jump...yeah, and Bella and Celeste, they just...they loved that. They loved jumping that high. It was amazing. Yeah. And then I went to see my grandma, my dad's mom...*

But the footage we have of Myrtle Beach doesn't look amazing at all. The sun isn't shining and the disconnect between Shan'ann [who's shooting video once again] and Watts is palpable. Even Shan'ann's father is there,** wandering awkwardly on the beach between the two warring parties. There's also a clear disconnect between Watts, standing like a big ape on the beach, and his daughters. Neither of them want to, though. When he does hold Bella's hand, she's simply standing there and so is he, neither engaging with the other.

One YouTuber, referring to this footage, suggests it's difficult to believe Watts would kill his children just a week later, but I think the opposite is true. He's already feeling the schlep of being a dad, and the discomfort of being back to the usual bullshit – being filmed against his will by his wife, and becoming little more than an extra in another one of her promos. If some people see this as an idyllic setting, Watts clearly didn't. In fact in that moment he's probably registering just how much he *doesn't* want to be there, and doesn't want to be part of the fake family *spiel* that simply won't come to an end.

Just as in a photo of him by the trampoline, although Watts is physically there, he doesn't seem to be there in the moment at all. So this description he's giving to Lee is totally disingenuous. One doesn't need to be a Rocket Scientist to see that. And what we're interested in here isn't so much the duplicity, we're not trying to check whether he's lying, we know he is. What we're interested in is trying to see how he crafts his self-reinforcing fairy tale, and how Lee lets him dig a hole for himself.

Here, at noon on Wednesday August 15th, it's already extremely weird that with his pregnant wife and two children missing for two days, Watts doesn't reflect on that at all during his tedious and time consuming reminiscing. There's no urgency, there's no concern, and yet he's asking the agent to believe that he cares about his family through his half-baked anecdotes of an amazing vacation and awesome trip to the beach. No real-time emotion or concern leaks through, and he has no suggestions – even when reflecting – on what could have happened, or what could be happening, based on recent history. Reality simply doesn't penetrate his wash of summer with the kids.

Watts seems to be overthinking his scheme. He knows they know that a separation was on the cards, which he thinks gives him a little leeway to be casual about his concern for them. He's concerned but there's a sort of resignation about it. Well, this resignation speaks volumes, doesn't it?

Within Watts' narrative, Shan'ann is placed on a kind of mute. Anything she says or does is excised from the story. He's also unable to connect the recent past to the present, in fact, what he's doing is try to *break all the relevant connections*. He's selectively leaving out all the stuff that matters, and so influencing the cops in an effort to exonerate himself.

It's almost incomprehensible that Watts is waffling on like this with the polygraph equipment hovering over his shoulder the whole time. A lawyer would have told him to shut up and just answer questions, but Watts reckons he's smart enough to manipulate the other person, the other woman, in the room. He isn't. And the price he pays for failing to sell his fairy tale, is that – in a few hours – he will find himself in a nightmare. Every word he is saying is a step in the direction of a cage. Once inside there is no coming out. He will spend decades in that cage if he's lucky, and eventually die in it. But this is how it starts, with the insistence of a fairy tale and an agent with a clip board smiling and asking for more detail.

*Discovery Documents, page 2074.

**Based on some photos, it appears <u>Sandi Rzucek was at Myrtle Beach</u> on that first day as well.

Introversion Exposed

"It is a joy to be hidden, and disaster not to be found." — D.W. Winnicott

Ernest Becker compares introversion to impotency in *The Denial of Death*. Becker's probably not referring strictly to impotence in the sexual sense, but if we assume he is, we find ourselves in a strange contradiction. Rather than impotent, Watts seemed to have a ravenous sexual appetite.

Even if we discount those [a man and several women] who claimed they had sex with Watts, and in one case a threesome including Shan'ann [Discovery Document, page 785], the *CBI Report* [page 5] quotes Watts saying Kessinger wanted to have sex all the time.

Kessinger herself told her friend Charlotte Nelson, sex with Watts was <u>the best sex she ever had</u>. We won't go into the possible implications behind Kessinger's Google searches ["how to prepare for anal sex"] hours before her final date with Watts, except to say Watts' sex life appeared far from impotent, or for that matter, introverted.

Becker also refers to the "self-awareness" that develops as a result of introversion. He describes it as becoming troublesome, especially within the context of family, and work. Becker writes about an "ulcerous gnawing" in response to an introverts "embeddedness", along with "a feeling of slavery in one's safety".

Watts was a passive, inert sufferer for much of his life, and most of his marriage. Whatever – or whoever – he was dreaming about, he did so in secret.

As Becker puts it:

"[But the introvert] can also assert himself out of defiance of his own weakness...[becoming] the master of his fate, a self-created man. He will not be merely a pawn of others, of society; he will not be a passive sufferer and secret dreamer, nursing his own inner flame in oblivion. He will plunge into life..."

To understand this crime and the man inside it, and the how and the why, we must get to grips with the psychology of introversion. Most of us think we know what it is. It's the opposite of extroversion. It's a person who doesn't say much. Yes, but it's much deeper than that. When we see Watts as an introvert, we're not necessarily seeing Watts or introversion. And we need to see both.

It's easy to be dismissive about it, as if introversion is a sort of lesser man, and a less impressive man. It might be. Becker describes the introvert as "basically weak" and "in a position of compromise", as well as "not an immediate man and not a real man either". Given these less than impressive and less than flattering descriptions and depictions, we can see why the default setting for someone in a relationship [including a friendship] with an introvert may be somewhat dismissive of them.

Becker describes the introvert as preferring to live a kind of incognito existence. Becker describes the introvert "toying" with concepts of who he'd rather be [and presumably, who he'd rather be with]. The introvert's response to being dismissed is, not surprisingly, to be somewhat dismissive of those around him. In time he cultivates a kind of "vaguely felt superiority" as Becker puts it. As it happens, these words perfectly describe Watts when he is being interrogated for hours by any number of agents and cops. Although polite and good-humored, Watts is somewhat dismissive of them because somewhere inside himself, he feels superior to them. If this seems a stretch, exactly the same feeling is mirrored in his interrogators. Watts is dismissed in the sense of being innocent or decent, but this dismissiveness and superiority is carefully hidden away, so that there is a *pretence* of "being on the same level". Of course Watts is also pretending to be on the same level, pretending to be honest, pretending all sorts of things.

That same hypocrisy is present in Watts' marriage, and even in his affair with Kessinger. Because what's really going on is a kind of unacknowledged *class war*. One might say it started with Shan'ann, who felt when she met Watts that he wasn't her type. He didn't look right and didn't dress right either.

Shan'ann was not impressed with him because he came to the date very underdressed... [Discovery Documents, page 582].

That feeling was apparently reciprocated by Cindy Watts, who felt Shan'ann wasn't right for her son, or simply didn't like the fact that Shan'ann would make insulting jabs about him to her behind his back.* Irrespective of whose side we are on [and *Rocket Science* needs to try to avoid taking sides], we can see how in the unfolding of the marriage, Shan'ann's superiority [if not contempt] for Watts became more manifest as the marriage went on. And vice versa.

The class war between Shan'ann and her husband spilled over into a war between herself and his parents, which in one rant she described to him as stupid and evil. It may not seem like a class war, but in her rant Shan'ann clearly sees herself and her children as superior – or simply better – than Watts' parents. Near the end of her rant Shan'ann wrote:

Our kids deserve the same love and attention the other kids get.

It's not clear whether this is reference to Jamie's kids, or other kids in general, but there's clearly a feeling of being compartmentalized here, and Shan'ann compartmentalizing his parents as part of an unsafe, and evil world. It seems excessive.

In Watts' affair with Kessinger there is also a class war. The weird thing is that it begins as a sort of inversion. Kessinger appears to be smitten not so much by Watts but by the portrait of his life. It's the whole fairy tale that beguiles her, including the big house. She's impressed by it. But as she gets to know him, the scales tip and the tables turn. In a purely blue-collar sense, he's from a rougher neighborhood, and a less educated background, and a lower class background, than she is. She's middle class. He's trying to be part of the middle class [and failing].

And of course there's the dimension of the class war through the prism of Thrive, which promises all its converts a better lifestyle. Put a patch on your arm, drink this shake, use this powder, and suddenly you go from being this class of person to this class. Suddenly you can own a flashy car, live a lavish lifestyle and go on exotic holidays [like people who are from a particular class]. It's very compelling. It's very tempting. It's a powerful ruse.

Finally, there's the dimension of the class war fought between the elites controlling the oil majors [and oil fields], and the ordinary community of Colorado – the folks in the suburbs. The oil companies claim to represent the needs of the many, and vocally represent populist but simplistic agendas like jobs, and job security. But there is absolutely no way the corporate titans sitting in their skyscrapers have the interests of the blue-collar folk at heart, unless it is to gather tens of thousands of lives and make sure the way these lives are directed [or misdirected] is good for the bottom-line, for profits.

So we see, from top to bottom, a kind of class war going on between spouses in a marriage, between families, between co-workers, and within the machinery of corporations, the justice system and entire communities in Colorado. Within this enormous and enormously complex dynamic, we have this strange snake called introversion slithering about. Although the snake is low, it carries with it the confidence of a lethal poison in its fangs. The snake [and I'm not saying all introverts are snakes, simply that this is how the psychology operates in true crime] creates *a distance between himself and the average man.*

August 7th:

"He hasn't touched me all week, kissed me, talked to me except for when I'm trying to figure out what is wrong... He's been distant since I left." [Discovery Documents, page 2105].

August 9th:

"He's talking and kinda being Chris... but he's very distant still."

August 15th [following the polygraph test]:

[Lee] told [Watts] [she] found it hard to believe he and Shan'ann had an emotional conversation...where they were both crying and he had yet to shed one tear in the 2 days [they] interviewed him. [Watts] said he loved his girls and it didn't mean anything that he hadn't shed any tears.

But of course it did mean something. It does mean something when we don't shed tears. It means our connections to those we love, or those we're supposed to love, are subverted – are INVERTED. This comes naturally to the introvert – subversion, undermining, disrupting, reversing, overturning. All these things sound negative, sound criminal, but they aren't necessarily. Some of the most heroic and talented men and women in the history of the world were/are introverts.

Bill Gates [Microsoft]

J.K. Rowling

Steven Spielberg

Theodor Seuss Geisel [Dr. Seuss]

Elon Musk [SpaceX, Tesla]

George Lucas

Larry Page [Google]

Abraham Lincoln

Hillary Clinton

Warren Buffett

Meryl Streep

Mark Zuckerberg [Facebook]

Neil Armstrong

Steve Wozniak [Apple]

Roy Orbison

Albert Einstein

Barack Obama

We tend to have an immediate like or dislike for some people on this list, just as some may have an immediate feeling of attraction or repulsion for Donald Trump. Much of this response speaks not only to our own level of introversion vis-à-vis these people, but also our place in society [our class] relative to theirs.

Many of these famous names deserve a deep dive into their backstories, but we're going to go into only one, the only rock star in the group. *Rolling Stone* put Roy Orbison at number 13 on their "Greatest Singers of All Time" list.

Clearly, courting crowds of screaming fans, being on stage and being famous is anathema to being shy and introverted. Singing itself feels like a complete contradiction to the idea of the quiet introvert. One might even say Roy Orbison couldn't *really* have been an introvert if he decided to become a musician, a performer. Isn't the litmus test for an introvert that they don't perform, that they shy away from the stage?

In the same way we may say Watts wasn't *really* an introvert if he had an affair, if he could hold court with the cops for hours on end, if he could brazenly conduct an affair at work let alone commit triple murder. But that's a mistake, and it shows we still don't understand how introversion works, or how real it is. So let's step into this oblivion and see what lies behind it.

Wikipedia provides a generic sketch specifically of the introverted aspect of Orbison's personality:

Orbison eventually developed a persona and an image that did not reflect his personality. He had no publicist in the early 1960s, therefore he had little presence in fan magazines…Life called him an "anonymous celebrity".

Orbison, who wore prescription glasses, started performing *purposefully* with dark glasses in 1963, not so much because he was trying to be cool, but because he had to. In so doing Orbison became one of the first pop stars to do so, long before the likes of Michael Jackson, U2's Bono and Lady Gaga.

Back to Wikipedia:

After leaving his thick eyeglasses on an airplane in 1963, while on tour with the Beatles, Orbison was forced to wear his prescription Wayfarer sunglasses on stage and found that he preferred them. His

NICK VAN DER LEEK

*biographers suggest that although he had a good sense of humor and was never morose, **Orbison was very shy and suffered from severe stage fright**; wearing **sunglasses helped him hide** somewhat from the attention.*

So Orbison's trademark sunglasses actually happened by accident, rather than design. He wasn't trying to be cool, a flaw was *misinterpreted* as cool. But to get a real sense of just how crazy the misunderstanding was, initially, between the reluctant performer and a quizzical audience, check this out:

*The ever-present sunglasses led some people to assume that **the stationary performer was blind**. [But] his black clothes and the desperation in his songs [conveyed] the image of mystery and introversion. His dark and brooding persona, combined with his tremulous voice in lovelorn ballads marketed to teenagers, made Orbison a star in the early 1960s.*

Orbison was such a hit, even the likes of Elvis called Orbison the greatest and most distinctive voice he'd ever heard. In 2012, Bruce Springsteen fleshed out the portrait even further:**

"[Orbison] was the true master of the romantic apocalypse you dreaded and knew was coming after the first night you whispered 'I Love You'…You were going down. Roy was the coolest uncool loser you'd ever seen. With his Coke-bottle black glasses, his three-octave range, he seemed to take joy sticking his knife deep into the hot belly of your teenage insecurities."

There was a hot belly of insecurity. While on tour, Orbison's wife started an affair with a contractor working on their home in Hendersonville, Tennessee. Those who knew Claudette, Orbison's wife, attributed the breakdown of their marriage to loneliness and boredom. Although the couple reconciled again, Claudette's infidelity continued, and they divorced for a second time the following year. One would imagine Orbison – the rising rock star – would be cheating and divorcing, not his wife, but he's the introvert, not her. They remarried, but the third marriage was cut short by a tragic accident in June 1966, when Claudette, while riding a motorcycle, smashed into the door of pickup truck which had turned in front of her. She died instantly.

Two years later, in 1968, while touring England, Orbison learned his home in Hendersonville had burned to the ground, the inferno consuming his two eldest sons. In March 1969 Orbison married a German teenager, Barbara Jakobs. He met Jakobs only a few days after his sons' deaths. Ten years later, in 1978, Orbison – who'd been a heavy smoker since he was a teenager – had a triple bypass. After the operation, he continued smoking.

Orbison's career hit a low ebb for much of the 80's, but towards the end of the decade he made an amazing comeback. Orbison lost some weight to suit his revived image. *Rolling Stone* wanted to spend several days with him, and there was talk of a book and a biopic. *Mystery Girl* was finalized in November 1988, and climbing the charts. Despite suffering chest pains, Orbison headed to Europe to accept an award. He did a show in Antwerp, Belgium, and started giving a series of interviews.

On December 6th, he spent a day flying model airplanes with his children, and had dinner with his mother in Hendersonville. He died that same day of a heart attack. Orbison was just 52-years-old. Remember the German teenager he'd married, seemingly on a whim, almost twenty years earlier? Barbara Jakobs was still married to him.

There's a lot to take out of Orbison's story, but the ambit of *OBLIVION* is to analyse and understand Chris Watts, so we'll limit our analysis to that. For starters, we see that Orbison himself wasn't fickle, superficial or shallow. When he got married he stayed married. Even when his wife cheated on him and divorced him, he tried to make it work. This feels like anathema to most other rock and roll celebrities. We may say that a true introvert feels deeply, and also that he loves deeply. Based on Orbison's music alone, Bruce Springsteen is spot on. He is the master of the romantic apocalypse, not because of a fluke, not serendipitously, but because he's lived it, experienced it.

Now, the other aspect we want to look at his Orbison's seemingly reckless romance with a German teenager in the middle of a serious family tragedy. This seems to convey the opposite, the notion that Orbison didn't feel very deeply, and didn't – or couldn't grieve – his own children. It's against this background that it's surprising, even shocking, that Orbison made his marriage work, and evidently so did she.

The takeout from this, into the Watts case is simply that we shouldn't dismiss the romantic apocalypse that was his failed relationship with Kessinger, on account of him being an introvert. It's the opposite. It's the fact that he's an introvert that makes his relationship with Kessinger a hot belly of angst, insecurity, sex and yes, love. Kessinger told him she loved him, and though their summer of love was short, like Orbison's romance with Barbara Jakobs, that doesn't mean it wasn't real to both of them.

Springsteen talks about *[taking] joy...sticking his knife deep into the hot belly,* he's not only describing the abortion Watts sought of his unborn son, or the painful ecstasy of new love, and a lot of great sex, he's also describing something we've been blind to from the start:

the joy of the introvert stumbling through his own insecurities, and finding a whole new side to himself, a whole, new, viable world in someone else.

*There are numerous examples of <u>Shan'ann openly criticizing Watts</u> on social media.

**Excerpt from Bruce Springsteen's <u>keynote address</u> at the SXSW festival in 2012.

Alienation

"It is an easy mistake to think that non-talkers are non-feelers." — *Wallace Stegner*

Now that we have some idea of dimensions of the introvert [these can be epic], we have to put them into some kind of perspective. How does it play out in true crime, and how are the strings of the introvert pulled that has any bearing on criminal psychology?

The human animal uses the process of thought to control his internal world. He puts various objects and symbols and meanings in place, and tries to steer himself away from anxiety and towards those things that enhance his self-esteem. But sometimes a situation is binary, and also – a bind. There may be no easy way out, or no way out whatsoever. This is the situation of an alienated or imprisoned individual. He is in a given situation against his will, and he soon develops an *us versus them* psychology.

The problem many introverts encounter in their ordinary lives is that they discover they're easily controlled, dismissed, bullied and manipulated. They're *expendable*. This is especially true when an introvert engages romantically, or through marriage. Orbison was treated like that, as a mere consolation prize by his first wife.

Watts felt like a consolation prize for much of his marriage. In one of her videos Shan'ann admits to not treating him well for a long time, but him sticking around "because he was the one for me". At times, Kessinger felt the same way; she felt she would always play "second fiddle" in Watts' life. She had no idea how *untrue* that would turn out to be.

When we dismiss the quietness of the introvert as emotional quietness, as non-feeling, we make a big mistake. It's the opposite. Introverts have so much held in, held back, stewing, they're capable of a much richer [and sometimes more destructive] inner life than other people. They feel so much they're sometimes incapable of expressing it. It's not that the feelings aren't there, it's that there's a stuttering difficulty to do due diligence to what's steaming inside. This is why the sociopathy label with Watts doesn't quite fit.

If he's a heartless monster, how was he able to love Kessinger the way he did, and vice versa? If he's a heartless monster, why is he such a bad liar; why are so many micro expressions leaking? Why does he cross his arms and sway when stressed, if he's not feeling anything? Why did Shan'ann still want to stay married to him, if he was so incapable of love and supposedly so unfeeling? And why would his mother and father profess unconditional love to him, after the crimes. If he'd never shown loved or affection or emotion to his parents, why did they feel he was deserving of love in *some* capacity?

Niko, the third child in the Watts family, also seemed to be a sort of consolation prize conceived to pull the couple out of their alienation for one another.

A consolation prize, when it fails to provide comfort, is expendable. I think in some ways Watts was that to Shan'ann. She found consolation in her children, and in Thrive, in her fellow promoters, in her big house, in the Lexus and through her phone. As she was progressively consumed by these things, these other objects, Watts felt increasingly alienated. He'd become little more than a monthly pay check, a sideshow extra, someone who did the laundry.

Ernest Becker describes alienation as:

"...first and foremost, the overshadowing of the organism by the object."

Shan'ann on her phone or on Facebook was one way *the organism* felt himself overshadowed.

We can say that Shan'ann experienced alienation from her husband as soon as *she* was overshadowed by the [new] sex object. Kessinger was that, and the many nude selfies reinforces this notion, but she was also much more. She represented a new life, a sustainable alternative, and a bright new future where Watts could be himself and feel himself acknowledged. After years of being overshadowed by Shan'ann, and more recently by her relentless pursuit of Thrive…

I knew she was in control…I knew what [laughs] my role was…I hated…being… in those [videos], I mean…"

…his romance with Kessinger had to feel like relief, excitement, adventure, a new lease on life, a big break from the usual anxiety, and a huge self-esteem boost, all rolled into one.

At the same time that this felt really good to Watts, now Shan'ann felt alienated. She felt how Watts now no longer acknowledged her, and didn't acknowledge her child. It's unkind – and unfair – to say, but through this experience of not being acknowledged, she was getting a dose of her own medicine. And whenever Watts favored Shan'ann over Kessinger,* she'd feel alienated. This would prompt her to Google topics such as "married man marry his mistress".

There is also the pregnancy itself, this promise of new life for a family, but also the end of a promising new life somewhere else, with someone else.

Becker also goes further, quoting Marx, when he writes:

"...to divorce oneself from action, to shun total individual involvement, is to condemn oneself to alienation..."

When a person isn't fully involved, and especially when he consents to being a limited version of himself, this is the beginning of alienation. We know that in the most basic sense, Watts was a self-limiting personality, and that Shan'ann was a controlling, and domineering character. We can see how both Shan'ann and Watts condemned him to an alienated version of himself, until Thrive transformed him, and then Kessinger's influence made him feel as if he could suddenly, magically, transcend his situation.

Watts' solution to the impasse he found himself in was action. Introverts are capable of action, and although they are unimpressive in what they do on a day-to-day basis, they are capable of defying themselves, and the world.

On July 4ᵗʰ Kessinger went to [Watts'] home in Frederick, Colorado to help [him] set up his diet and weight loss goals. Kessinger said this was the first time she was at Watts' home. After spending time at [his] home [Kessinger] went to the Colorado Rockies baseball game without [him]...[Discovery Documents, page 647]. The *CBI Report* [page 25] provides additional context to this:

[Watts] woke up the morning of July 4, 2018, at Kessinger's house because he didn't have to work that day. When he woke up, he had 10 missed calls from Shan'ann. He went outside [to call her back]...and Shan'ann was "pissed."... [She] yelled at him and asked him where he was at...and hung up on him. He

went back inside [Kessinger's home] and told [her] he had to go home in case Shan'ann called back. Kessinger asked him if he was going to come back and he said no. Kessinger was "pissed" he left.

Four days later Kessinger, still feeling sensitive about the incident, Googled topics related to "marrying your mistress". [Discovery Documents, page 2106].

Amalgamation

*"There are no clear borders, Only merging invisible
to the sight." — Dejan Stojanovic*

It's no exaggeration to say there's a proportional relationship between money and self-esteem. There's also a similar proportional
relationship between love and self-esteem. Money and love are also
related, which is why wealthy men – even beasts – are able to attract
beauties, and poor men, even deserving true men, are not.

Lots of money, lots of self-esteem. Lots of love, lots of self-esteem.

Lots of love and money = the contrivance of fairy tales.

Little money, little love, dangerously low self-esteem = the shatter-
ing of fairy tales.

See, it's when self-esteem is dangerously low, or under threat, that
the anxiety/ego dynamic comes into play. The anxiety magnifies –
leverages – the ego, and the ego does its damnedest to rescue the organism from its symbolic malaise.

I want to start by comparing *the marriage, the situation of the mistress, and the pregnancy* – all three of these *dimensions* – to a much
larger canvas playing out in Colorado at the same time as the Watts
Family Murders. In August 2018, America and Anadarko were enjoying a crude oil bonanza, and as a permutation of this summer of excess,

this season of excess, Anadarko was being wooed by <u>Chevron Corp</u>, America's third largest <u>Oil Major</u>.

According to <u>*Bloomberg*</u> [June 7th, 2019]:

Chevron Corp. just kept saying no [to Anadarko].

Effectively, Chevron was wooing Anadarko, and Anadarko was communicating a few things:

1. It was ready and available. [It wanted to be wooed, but it also wanted to be wanted].

2. It felt undervalued. [It wanted more].

3. Anadarko was asking Chevron to express a deeper commitment. [It wanted a bigger wedding ring].

Are people so mercenary, so merciless?

Bloomberg reports on a "much longer effort" by <u>Occidental</u>, to acquire Anadarko. This effort began in July 2017.

…CEO Vicki Hollub reached out to express interest. A few months later, the company sent a formal letter offering $61.22 a share, a 23% premium at the time.

Now, if we *insist* on <u>anthropomorphizing</u> this corporate dalliance any further, we can say that of the two companies flirting for Anadarko's hand, Occidental was the more committed suitor. Occidental did the proper thing and formally expressed interest, and Anadarko rejected the bid. Al Walker, Anadarko's CEO expressed reservations about the proposal. Anadarko just didn't like the way Occidental was dressed and didn't think the "proposed combination" would work. In other words, Walker was acting a little like Cindy Watts, or Shan'ann, in the early dating days.

Anadarko hesitation, broadly speaking, made sense. Chevron was bigger and more established. It made more sense to play hard to get for a spell, and see if Chevron would come round.

But Occidental wouldn't take no for an answer, and in January 2018 increased their offer by $15 to a $76 per share offer. Although Anadarko also rejected this offer, the board made a suggestion. If Occidental could make it an all-cash deal, they'd be willing to get into bed with Oxy.

And then things went quiet through the rest of 2018.

Why?

Well, Chevron had snuck in from the side, but now Anadarko really had the hots for Occidental. In March 2019, a few days after the Second Confession and effectively the closure of the Watts case [legally speaking and otherwise], Occidental repeated the original $76-a-share bid. The fact that Occidental's offer had been frozen at the same price for a year speaks volumes. It was as if *something* had intruded onto the canvas, and frozen the whole process. And then in March 2019, it unfroze.

The thaw, when it happened, was rapid. According to *Bloomberg*:

A month later [in April], [Occidental's CEO] Hollub reduced her offer price to $72, but boosted the cash portion. Three days after that, on April 11, she changed her mind and reverted back to $76, with 40% cash and the offer of board seats for Walker and two other Anadarko directors. By that evening, however, Anadarko signed its deal with Chevron.

The predicted merger of two of the three companies was going to be like a marriage. But at the same time, another player came along, a mistress – Chevron. The "pregnancy" keeping these "players" in a bind, was Proposition 112, and obviously the gyrations of larger macroeconomics, especially oil prices. It's also possible the negative publicity of the Watts case could have caused a massive dampener on share offers had these continued through late 2018. Think about it. Had the Watts case come into its own through a fully-fledged, fire breathing criminal case laying siege to the airwaves of Colorado for weeks on end, the damaging PR [related two Anadarko oil workers] would eventually develop the capacity to scorch the iron thrones of the Permian and turn pots of gold under the mountains to ash. The Watts case in August 2018 had the mettle to become not only the highest-profile true crime case in America, but possibly *ever*.

But what if the affair could be put on the backburner for a while, until the harsh winds blew over?

We see a long period of flirtation and then entanglement, with Occidental eventually emerging after a hiatus, and sort of proving itself as marriage material, while the mistress – Chevron – hovered, creating a kind of suspense.

Bloomberg calls the takeover of Anadarko "a rare example of a public bidding war involving large oil companies…" It is that. But consider the lexicon. A *takeover*. When large companies marry, they don't remain two separate entities. One engulfs the other. One literally swallows the other, the smaller company ceases to exist in name, and in many other respects.

What does industrial society tell us about ourselves? Industrial society brings new corporate entities into being, but these are still institutions built and run by men. How does this "takeover" psychology inform ordinary people, especially those who work for these giant companies? Isn't it the idea that what is loved can also be consumed? And so what is loved is also expendable. Is there a psychological feedback mechanism where the dynamics of the company filter into the dynamics of its drones? And the dynamic is this: What is loved can and should be eaten and engorged, because the only motive is the profit-movie, I/me *uber alles*. My self-esteem at the expense of everything else, just name your price, and make sure it's the right price.

For Watts the right price appeared to be a house and a mistress. The murders were his way of taking over, to make himself amendable – the right bid – to her.

Bloomberg concludes:

*Chevron's decision **not to raise its offer in response to Occidental is what cleared the way for the biggest acquisition of an oil producer in four years**. In the end, **Anadarko would pay a $1 billion termination fee** to end that deal in favor of Occidental's proposal.*

We can compare Chevron's decision not to raise its offer to Shan'ann accepting the inevitability of a breakup rather than committing to a battle:

"Fuck him!...I will fight for full custody..."

Or we can compare Chevron's letting go to Kessinger not sending all those nude selfies, especially when Watts was in North Carolina. When he returned, she may have rejected his offer to take her to the Lazy Dog restaurant, and not had sex with him before and after.

On the other hand, Shan'ann's response to fight for her marriage did the opposite of clearing the way for Kessinger, it blocked it. The pregnancy, just like the Watts case, was going to burn the house down, it was going to be unaffordable PR to two giant fire-breathing entities that wanted to live, wanted to be all they could be, and wanted to merge. The pregnancy – just like the catastrophic PR a criminal trial threatened – blocked, limited and burned away the possibility of an acquisition.

As I've noted, the huge house was Watts' ticket to a new life. It was in his name, and there was enough treasure to get from it if he could get his hands on it. But the PR of the pregnancy was standing in his way, as was Shan'ann, and his little girls. The only way out was to take control, to turn his family into oil.

Phantom Zone

"It is far harder to kill a phantom than a reality."
—Virginia Woolf

Though he was <u>in dire financial straits</u>, he didn't seem to care. This is either an appearance of carelessness [with regard to the finances] or actual carelessness, and possibly both. Which is it?

It seems Watts was aware of his financial conundrum but locked out of it. That didn't stop him from using the Anadarko gift cards until they were exhausted, or credit cards for unnecessary purchases [wining and dining his mistress], or dipping into the expense account for unnecessary expenses [hiring a babysitter so he could go out and spend money on his mistress]. If Watts was aware of being locked out, he had to imagine how doing a divorce the proper way would leave him high and dry.

Watts was obviously in love when his first priority should have been figuring out his finances. He should have been trying to find a viable way out of his debt trap, not his marriage, but maybe they're not so easy to separate. Maybe they were one and the same.

Regardless, Watts focus wasn't where it should have been; he was trying to make every moment of freedom count while he had it, and making every penny count in terms of paying the bills of the affair.

NICK VAN DER LEEK

In this sense he really was living in a dream world. There was only so much money and he seemed prepared to spend the very last cent lying in the cracked belly of the piggybank, before cycling over to deal with the next crisis.

Of course on the day *after* her death, the piggybank was due to receive some sort of injection from Le-Vel, though we have no idea how much, or what these amounts – this income – typically were. Watts may also have wanted to get his paws on that, in addition to the house and his happily ever after in the great, glittering beyond that lay in the tragedy's aftermath.

Given Watts' record with the truth, and Shan'ann's history with MLM, it's probable that they both knew what was happening, they knew about the finances and *did* care. Shan'ann seemed aware of the prospect of moving house before August 12th,* and perhaps this prospect alone was the reason for the "last ditch" promotional effort in North Carolina.

It's also possible that magical thinking had somehow interfered with rational thinking, and so it wasn't a case of not caring in terms of their finances, but believing in fairy tales that they would *somehow* end happily ever after. The murders themselves feel like a dark and perverse form of magical thinking. Diabolical magic, dark magic, but magic all the same.

It's hard to care about a pregnancy, or to acknowledge one's obligations, when you're ensconced in an affair.

It's hard to care about debt when you're drowning in excess, and that was one of the central promises of Thrive. Fancy cars, fancy lifestyle, free time, free holidays, make a fortune by gabbing to your pals all day about how happy you are on Facebook. Get drunk on the Kool-Aid you're selling.

Since Shan'ann was still committed to Thrive right up to the final hours of her life [arguably more committed to Thrive than to her marriage], we can see how she was invested completely in a narrative of hope, or cracking one more sale, and reaching the next bar on the Thrive jungle gym.

When the foreclosure notices arrive, you tend to notice things. The anxiety starts to lift upward in a steep learning curve before the inevitable crisis and crash. The fact that they'd already gone through one bankruptcy, and the fact that Shan'ann had already been through a divorce, meant both Watts and Shan'ann were primed to panic, but in very different ways, and in very different areas. Shan'ann wanted to make her marriage work, at all costs. Watts wanted not to lose everything he'd worked his whole life for, at all costs.

One does care – realistically – about debt when you start losing things. When those limits kick in, when the ATM bleats impassively TRANSACTION DENIED, INSUFFICIENT FUNDS, then the debt situation manifests as an extremely limiting cage. Panic sets in. Before that happens, debt, even serious debt, can seem like a mere construct at first, like a harmless hypothetical, a fiction rather than a reality. Far more real are one's own demands, one's own material needs day to day. If one credit card maxes out there's always another. As long as there's another, self-esteem wins the day and anxiety can be kept at bay. But once the time is up on that score, the seesaw whips the other way pretty quick, doesn't it?

Debt can feel paralyzing, so real when it comes home to roost, it threatens to *take* your home, and engulf everyone and everything you own. It feels like drowning, dying, fading into oblivion. That's about as real as it gets.

The large MLM phantom zone that is the backdrop to this case is *all* about self-esteem. It's all about Thrivin'. Ironically, so is the profit-oriented boom or bust world of Anadarko. If it's all about enjoying a bigger, better lifestyle and winning a slimmer, more improved, more attractive version of oneself, where does that raw transactionality come from? What drives these binary equations? Big Oil. It's all or nothing, sink or swim, my way or the highway.

Corporates are also interested in fairy tales, and fairy tale endings. When one corporate wins big, a lot of little companies crumble to dust and go out business. That's commerce. But it's not just commerce, it's a psychology, and arguably a criminal one at that. According to Becker:

"...alienation exists when man objectifies himself vis-a-vis abstract thought or symbols..."

Where does he learn to do that? From big companies, brands, branded products...a machine-world. The whole of Shan'ann's day each day was a festival of branding herself and objectifying her family to make money. MLM is a turn off for good reason. It turns people into products and promoters. MLM objectifies everything. Consider how Thrive objectifies life itself. Each moment is monetised. Each intimacy is taken over and rendered inauthentic, and impersonal.

A selfie that's been photoshopped is the classic description of the modern everyday attempts to objectify ourselves as unrealistic fairy tales. Facebook and social media as a whole is about reducing human being to symbols, statuses, avatars, memes, numbers and "profiles". Ideas and existence itself can be reduced or quantified according to likes.

It's an easy narrative to contribute to. It's all about aesthetics, repeatedly quantifying, comparing and objectifying whatever is beautiful and expensive and aspirational. It's populist, it's tribal, and above all, it inflames our natural narcissism. We think aspiring endlessly is good, even inspiring, but it's not. We think expanded influence is good, but there's no end to it. How much is enough? Instead of community-ism, or social-ism, which is seen as evil, or threatening, we live in a system of money: capital-ism. This system sells the idea of MORE. That we deserve more than we have, and that we deserve to have more than we are, or can afford. Capital-ism tries to sell us a world that the world itself is not, and can't afford. It sells a fairy tale, at the cost of all, not only men, but mice, and mules, and meerkats.

In MLM, luxury cars and exotic holidays are part of the fairy tale package. All of these things can be yours if you simply snap your fingers and sign up to Thrive. Don't hold yourself back, *believe* and you can have it all! It is human nature to want the best for ourselves, and to aspire to a better life. But there is a reason we don't believe in *unbelievable* fairy tales. In corporate settings there's a cost to failing to honor a deal. Anadarko paid Chevron $1 billion for the right to say "no thanks", after saying "maybe". In the real world there's also a cost to peddling fairy tales.

Becker refers to a "central bureaucratic national state" which "allows neither individuality nor community". And this is the crux. Capital-ism, and corporates, and MLMs, and a binary approach where one thing consumes another, doesn't enhance individuality or community, it destroys both. What it does is it enhances itself. It's a kind of narcissism, but it's not narcissism, it's the ego run amok. Now the ego is not just a defense against anxiety, it's a defender of self-esteem.

Really? So 10 000 likes or followers can provide a person with real self-esteem? This is the new currency, and of course, it's a fairy tale.

Self-esteem *was* a central aspect, and a major artefact that spilled over from the phantom zone of Watts' childhood into adulthood. It had to do with the class he came from, and the class he was headed into. Precisely the same dynamic applied to Shan'ann. Self-esteem is both the kernel *causing* the spending and the cloud covering any attempt [or willingness] to deal with the debt as it began to manifest as real limits in real life.

Self-esteem is impinged – at least in this story – by *poverty*. Poverty is the antithesis of the fairy tale, and so it must be hidden. Just like the bankruptcy, and the broken marriage, poverty is shameful in a capital-ist society.

The excess we see when the couple move from North Carolina to Colorado, is the swing of the pendulum to the other extreme, just as the murders are an excessive swing from dutiful family man and father to a murdering free agent who's only in it for himself.

They *both* held the dogs of anxiety at bay by living beyond their means. They found their self-worth attached to the worth of stuff, and how stuff looked. The phantom zone of living beyond one's means is reflects the phantom zone of deprivation, of poverty. It's absolutely central to low self-esteem and the ego. It's a greed for more but without the capability to pay for it, much like the fabric** of this crime and this case.

*_Shan'ann had already contacted the realtor_ the week before... [Discovery Documents, page 593].

**Watts committed a serious crime but was unable to convincingly lie about it to get himself off the hook, or even when on the hook and serving his sentence, he *still* couldn't account for his actions. This is analogous to someone who can't afford something but buys it anyway. This makes the circumstances of the Watts case more than a little analogous to entire nations with crippling debt burdens and endless bailouts.

Oblivion

"You see a dead body and it's like, it's OK. He's gone. I don't want to be like him; I have to move on."— Mrika Nikqa, 17, from Kosovo

[Soundtrack for this chapter*]

Have you ever eaten sardines on toast? The toast pops out of the toaster and thin slices of butter are placed on the warm, singed surfaced. While the butter softens and melts, the can of sardines must be torn open. The top of the can has a lever like you get on a soda can. Twist it, and tear open the tin. It curls like a paper-thin banana peel. Inside the can are the corpses of three silver sardines [*Clupea Harengus*]. Three headless, tailless cadavers glistening in rapeseed oil.

Using a knife, spread the melted butter over the still-warm toast. Now fish out the first fish cadaver, dripping in oil, and transfer it to the toast. Put pressure on the cadaver. Crush its soft body, transform it from a fish body to a kind of paste. Spread its broken body over the butter and over the whole bread. Add a little salt. Now eat it.

OBLIVION is relative. If you're eating sardines on toast, something else's *OBLIVION* isn't bad at all. It might even taste good. But if you're the sardine, if *you're* that headless, tailless body that's ended up in a tin can, preserved in rapeseed oil, packaged as food with two other unfortunates just like you, no more and no less than a single small meal for a large giant, then *OBLIVION* is extremely unpleasant.

OBLIVION is the wall Watts is looking at while facing a polygraph test. With the clock ticking over his right shoulder, and various recording devices catching his every word, he projects onto this wall fictions and fairy tales as a way to escape his fate, to wriggle out of accountability. But there is no escape. Just like for the sardine, once those walls are around you, that's it, that's the end for you.

OBLIVION is the walls that surround him now at Dodge, and with each year, each decade, those walls seem to move in. There is no dodging those walls, no escape, no happy ending. There's just *OBLIVION*.

OBLIVION is an inevitable end result for us all. Those walls, those ears, are waiting and listening for us too. It's a terrifying prospect when we see it not as a hypothetical construct, but a real box in the real world. Whatever fairy tales we may construct to push anxiety back and protect our egos, those walls persist. Ultimately they will intrude into our reality, because the walls of *OBLIVION* are reality itself.

Through the Watts case we see a family broken into pieces. Each piece is placed in a box – like sardines – and each box placed into the ground. In Watts' case, the man behind it all is put inside a box above ground so that he may experience *OBLIVION* for the rest of his life. A living death, in other words.

"A few names have survived oblivion. In time, oblivion will have them all." — Marty Rubin

Imagine spending 10, 20, 30, perhaps even 40 years in a single cell. Imagine what it is to be a sardine. But there's something worse than being murdered. It's defaulting to an *OBLIVION* of your own making, and worse, condemning others to the same fate.

In the eight books that comprise this series, I've endeavoured to drill as deeply as possible into the minutiae of this case, but also expand the meaning of the Watts case to the largest possible canvas. The psychological tendrils reach far and wide, and if we're brave, we see them creeping through our own lives too, far beyond the strata of Colorado.

When we contemplate the annihilation of Shan'ann [who today is a skeleton in a graveyard, not a 30-something selling powders online], and the two little girls, and the grapefruit sized fetus that was expelled into a dusty grave [all these little lives now little more than dust and chalk in an oily box], we're contemplating our own, inevitable *OBLIVION*.

The Watts story is about unwanted spouses, unwanted children and holding grudges. It's a warning to us about the dangers of courting *OBLIVION* in our own lives. *OBLIVION* is a certainty, it waits for us in death, and the eternity of beyond death. The trick is to avoid *OBLIVION* as individuals, as communities, as societies, cultures and nations. Can we?

As taboo as the themes in the Watts case seem to be, they're quite common in the world. We don't see it and we don't hear about it, because people *hide* it. But it's there. It's everywhere. Take grudges. Grudges are a kind of symbolic *OBLIVION*, just as blocking someone on social media is that too. And haven't we all done that with impunity? Blocking on social media is so every day it's a cliché. We're so dehumanized, we know longer see real people behind those avatars, which is why they're so easy to treat like nothings and nobodies. That's how close *OBLIVION* is. It's right here in the fabric of society.

And so, with *OBLIVION* comes anxiety.

How do we respond to it? How should we respond?

We are outraged by the murders of innocent children, and the murder of a pregnant woman, and yet isn't our outrage much like that of the district attorney in this case? Michael Rourke is the face of the prosecution in this case. He's spoken about his outrage, and how the spotlight that needed to shine in this case, shone in the right place – not on Shan'ann, on Chris Watts.

"What I can tell you most affirmatively today, by what happened in the courtroom, is the spotlight that he tried to shine on Shan'ann falsely … has been corrected. The spotlight shines directly where it belongs: on him." [District Attorney Michael Rourke, November 6th, 2018, press conference following the announcement of a plea deal]

But that's not true. There was never a spotlight. The spotlight was destroyed. Even the spotlight in this case is a pretended spotlight. The reality of this case and investigation into it is *OBLIVION*. The reality of what happened is this story, but it is quite literally, as far as the real world is concerned, and legal reality – *OBLIVION*.

While this case promised to examine the wider issues of MLMs and oil companies, those narratives have been neatly filed and pushed into a drawer. The narrative of the case is Watts' final version which is to say, no narrative at all. And yet the figureheads of this case claim the final version is the decisive version, and that it's sufficient.

In the recent Investigation Discovery documentary, *Family Man, Family Murderer*, I couldn't help see *faux outrage* in the commentary of the prosecutor juxtaposed with the failure to actually prosecute or even make an effort to understand the perpetrator, one year down the line.

Just as Chris Watts said the right things, but wasn't acting right, and seemed too cold, <u>the prosecutor said exactly the right thing</u>, but wouldn't seem to act, <u>and seemed not to care as much as he ought to have done</u>. If the prosecutors' outrage isn't authentic, if it's acted in a court and for cameras rather than felt and followed through, and <u>if the parents are simply inheritors of the same MLM mechanisms</u> that fed into the original disaster, what hope is there for anyone in this world?

<u>The Watts case raises disturbing questions</u> not only about how individuals deal with individuals in a family, but how communities and cultures – and the media – deal with each other.

How do we dispose of people we don't agree with or don't like?

What does that do to the world and what does that do to us?

<u>Modern democracy has become a joke</u>, an unworkable joke. <u>Brexit</u>, <u>politics in America</u>, <u>South Africa</u>, <u>a joker becoming president in Ukraine</u> – all of these are simply the logical ends to modern capitalism and its mantras of consumerism and transactionalism. Capitalism without intervention becomes binary. It becomes about profit and loss, and nothing else. True crime is the same. One wins, the other loses, but the loser is purposefully taken out or taken over, just as companies do.

The point is the way societies are geared, and the way we as individuals are going, will have to change if we're to avoid *OBLIVION* in our lives, in this generation. The system of enslavement must be tinkered with, the settings and programs of the MegaMachines altered to acknowledge the personalities of human beings not at their expense, but to set them free to be who they are. What happens when people, systems and structures simply don't acknowledge other people, and their distinct personalities?

Watts told Kessinger that Shan'ann never let him openly communi-cate. [Kessinger] knew of no other stressors other than finances. [Watts] mainly complained that Shan'ann would never listen to him. Shan'ann would talk shit to him in front of his children and the children were start-ing to repeat it. When he tried to ask for something Shan'ann she said 'Shut up, you don't know anything'. His children started to repeat this and it made [him] very sad, and this is when he realized he needed to separate from her. [Discovery Documents, page 576].

So the solution is this: maximum individuality and maximum com-munity. Right now the problem is the opposite. We are being stripped of who we are as persons and as groups. Culture is no longer a reflec-tion of how we are, or how things are, but a kind of profit-oriented PR that is increasingly fake news.

How do we dispose of people we don't agree with or don't like?

What does that do to us?

The 2013 movie *OBLIVION* starring Tom Cruise addresses this ques-tion. We see the canvas of the world, and what *OBLIVION* looks like. Noth-ing human remains. There is no diversity, everything is in ruins, and the few individuals there are not individuals at all, but drones, cloned drones, drones repairing drones set forth in a scheme controlled by a distant and still deceitful machine intelligence. People aren't machines, but we've be-come machine-like, and binary in our views of ourselves and the world. Populism is binary. Tribalism is binary. And to be fair, it *feels* right. That's because dualism is natural. Some might even say it's innate.

As Becker puts it:

*"...there is a natural dichotomy between consciousness and the or-ganismic substratum out of which it develops – **a dichotomy which, when uncoordinated, will lead to mental illness."***

He's talking about social consciousness and Selfhood. If there is no Selfhood, if the self isn't authentic, we can see how the collective when expanded to billions, will manufacture enormous inauthentic systems and mechanisms that will dwarf and make a mockery of men – manipulate them, use them and if left unchecked, destroy them.

Destroy us.

It's happening.

It has to be undone.

In order for that to happen we have to become coordinated. We have to *be* coordinated. We have to be connected to ourselves and the world, and vice versa. We get our insides from society, and society is what it is because of us. But what have we become? Shallow. Superficial. Selfish. Expendable. Expendable as individuals and the expendable masses.

I first encountered this feedback loop when I studied James Howard Kunstler, a New Urbanist.

> *"We have created thousands and thousands of places in America that aren't* worth caring about, *and when we have enough of them, we're going to have a country that's not worth defending." — James Howard Kunstler*

Kunstler recognizes how people and communities who stop caring about themselves begin to construct urban environments that *don't care about us.* This is because they're built to the scale of machines – cars – rather than on the human scale. Soon we begin to feel alienated by the very environments we've built.

NICK VAN DER LEEK

We feel the reality of that side of the equation creeping rapidly up on us as we engage on social media, and create our own virtual custom-communities, and render groups in them intolerable and expendable. And then we find that we are too, not only to others, but to ourselves, expendable.

The Watts case is about a family unit seen through the greedy gaze of machine-eyes in the very same way: *as expendable*, and then, entangled in his own entanglements, strung up in his own string, the orchestrator, the puppet master, deems *himself* expendable. But at least he gets to hold onto the fairy tale. No one can take that away from him...

"It feels like a roller coaster ride that I just kept punching a ticket on and never could get off."**

That's the problem in his story and our story. Our fairy tales doom us to *OBLIVION* not at the end of our lives, but during – *in* – our lives; within our lifetimes. We're not escaping *OBLIVION* we're courting it. We're throwing away our lives, and we're so worn down when we realize what we've done, how much we've lost, we no longer care.

Our fairy tales are our *OBLIVION* unless they're authentic. There's nothing wrong with a fairy tale, as long it doesn't enslave us. It should inspire us, but with truth. Authentic fairy tales aren't reductionist, or exclusive. They're not binary – they're sustainable. They're genuine in the sense that they match a real individual to a real world. Their place in the world, and the world itself is genuine. Is that so hard to achieve?

It matters what human beings do because of our dominion over this world. If we lose ourselves, millions of creatures perish as well. We're responsible for them. We are responsible for this world and what happens to it. And so we *can't* believe ourselves or this world to be expendable. It's a precious planet, along with everything in it. A pin-prick of unfathomable abundance, surrounded by the vast gulf of space.

How do we dispose of people we don't agree with or don't like?

What is *OBLIVION*? It's the psychological shipwreck [consciousness] that is CERVI 319, but also the wrecked physical landscape [the organismic substratum], the broken bodies and minds buried inside it. The site itself, like Chris Watts, speaks to the derelict human condition.

CODER: *So once you get to the site, then what happens?*

As he drove to the oil site with Shan'ann, Bella and Celeste, he was nervous, shaking, and didn't know what was going to happen. He knew at that moment that his life was completely changed. He has tried to picture the long ride out to the oil site and wondered if he could have saved his girls' life. He wasn't thinking during the entire drive.***

This is a version of events that's meant to conceal reality in *OBLIVION*. But some parts of the *OBLIVION* are true. He was nervous. He didn't know what was going to happen. He did know his life had completely changed. But who changed his life? He did. Who could have saved all their lives? He could have.

How do we dispose of people we don't like?

He wakes up in the morning and goes to work, but that's not what's really happening. His work is his mistress, and he's disposing of his family, making them disappear into the vast fabric of Anadarko, his children into its chambers and tanks, his wife, the unborn child, buried in the dust of the ranch given over to the Oil Major.

"Merging like two drops of water. Together in a way that humans could never know." — L.J. Smith, Secret Vampire

Which brings us at last to the moment of truth.

Do you remember the question posed earlier in this narrative?

How was a violent triple murder committed without violence?

Are you sure you want to hear this?

But you already know the answer, don't you?

I was always somebody that tried to coax people down.

In other narratives we have seen the connection between Watts' perceived suffocation by society and how he chooses to kill his pregnant wife and daughters [at least in his version of events]. The *Rocket Science* version is he poisons his daughters early Sunday night and suffocates his wife the moment she arrives home and starts to ascend the staircase, perhaps using a rag soaked in ethanol covering her mouth to speed things up. This execution mirrors the way he's felt himself poisoned from within and strangled from without.

I was always somebody that tried to coax people down...just flying under the radar.

And then there's the disposal afterwards, the *OBLIVION* afterwards. What *OBLIVION* does Watts choose? He chooses the one he's most familiar with.

The landscape is empty except for two tanks. On a human scale, especially on the scale of a 4-year-old girl with small, budding, insect-like limbs, the tanks are enormous. But on the scale of the monotonous rolling landscape, the tanks are quite small. Even so, they stand out against the tawny fabric of sagebrush, cactus and yellow sunflowers.

He does not own any weapons, but nothing seemed right that morning...Time seemed to stand still and he saw his life disappearing before his eyes but he couldn't let go. He had wanted his whole life to be a dad and nothing made sense, including the oil tank.***

And as the great light of a new day spreads over the countryside, he parks his truck

When he gets to the oil site, he takes Shan'ann out of the back of the truck and pulls her over and lays her on the ground near where she was ultimately buried.***

Some of what he remembers is real, some of it what he wishes were true. He wishes they were still alive, and if they were, what they might say.

Bella said, "Daddy, it smells...What are you doing to mommy? Are you going to do to me what you did to mommy?"

He doesn't recall what he told them.***

Three dead females and an unborn male.

How do we dispose of people?

...coax people down... fly under the radar...

He forces her fragile, stick-like frame through the hatch. He presses his children, one by one through the holes, and hears them drop into a toxic, hot, liquid darkness below his feet. This is what he wants. This is what he must do to have his fairy tale. They will disappear into an *OBLIVION* of his own making. He can rely on the security of the well site to keep the prying eyes of the world away from here, keep them in the dark, *oblivious...*

After their bodies are dealt with, he will deal with their stories.

...coax people down... fly under the radar...

Like their bodies, he will simply put their story into a box, put a bow around it, and turn what really happened to them into a fairy tale.

I can sing you a song, take you home*

But I can't seem to find my own

I can sing you a song, take you home

But I can't seem to find my way home

*Lyrics from <u>Dido, Take You Home</u>.

**From page 4 of the *CBI Report.*

***From page 10 of the *CBI Report.*

About the Author

Nick van der Leek *[@HiRezLife on Twitter and @Nickvdk on Instagram] is a widely published photojournalist and the author of over 80 books, including several trilogies dedicated to unravelling the world famous, and still officially unsolved Jon-Benét Ramsey and Madeleine McCann cases. He has also travelled to France and the Netherlands to research the murder of Vincent van Gogh.*

Instead of journalism, Van der Leek studied law, economics and marketing. After two years cutting his teeth in a busy newsroom he became a full-time investigative writer. Today he is one of the most prolific true crime authors in the world.

He has sat in on many high-profile court cases, including Oscar Pistorius, Henri van Breda and Jason Rohde, and has occasionally advised criminal prosecutors during court cases on an extemporary basis. His research on the mysterious death of Vincent van Gogh has been added to the archives of the Van Gogh Library, in Nuenen, the Netherlands.

The ninth and final title in the TWO FACE series, EPILOGUE, deals with the vast troves of material collected during the research of the first eight books, but considered too minor to mention at the time of writing. EPILOGUE pieces together the final scenario of the crime in a final, definitive timeline that integrates all the evidence, and all the footage. It will also provide the final revelations and news updates in this case. The release of the final title will depend on the popularity of OBLIVION.

For more information on new releases, reviews, blogs and discussions, visit crimerocket.com.

Made in the USA
Monee, IL
19 December 2019